# A Cavalier's Note Book

LONDON : PRINTED BY
SPOTTISWOODE AND CO., NEW-STREET SQUARE
AND PARLIAMENT STREET

Fac-simile of a Commission, signed by Major-General Sir Thomas Tyldesley, appointing William Blundell to be Captain of one Company of Dragoons in his Regiment

# Crosby Records

A

# CAVALIER'S NOTE BOOK

BEING

*NOTES, ANECDOTES, & OBSERVATIONS*

OF

## WILLIAM BLUNDELL

*of Crosby, Lancashire, Esquire*

CAPTAIN OF DRAGOONS UNDER MAJOR-GEN. SIR THOS. TILDESLEY, KNT.
IN THE ROYALIST ARMY OF 1642

EDITED, WITH INTRODUCTORY CHAPTERS, BY THE

## REV. T. ELLISON GIBSON

AUTHOR OF

'LYDIATE HALL AND ITS ASSOCIATIONS'

## The Naval & Military Press Ltd

in association with

## The National Army Museum, London

*Published jointly by*

## The Naval & Military Press Ltd

Unit 10 Ridgewood Industrial Park,
Uckfield, East Sussex,
TN22 5QE England

Tel: +44 (0) 1825 749494
Fax: +44 (0) 1825 765701

www.naval–military–press.com
www.military–genealogy.com
www.militarymaproom.com

*and*

## The National Army Museum, London

www.national–army–museum.ac.uk

TO

# NICHOLAS BLUNDELL

*of Crosby, Lancashire, Esq., J.P., D.L.*

COLONEL OF DUKE OF LANCASTER'S OWN RIFLE MILITIA

THIS VOLUME

WHICH ENSHRINES SOME OF THE WISDOM
OF A WORTHY ANCESTOR

IS

Respectfully Inscribed

# CONTENTS.

—◦◦◦—

## CHAPTER III.

## CHAPTER IV.

---

## FRONTISPIECE.

# INTRODUCTORY.

———◆———

## CHAPTER I.

### THE BLUNDELLS OF CROSBY.

*The Blundells of Little Crosby in Lancashire—Seated first at Ainsdale—Of Norman descent—First charter temp. Henry II.—Remarks on seals—King John exchanges Ainsdale for Liverpool—Sir Robert Blundell, Knight, with Edward I. in Wales—Nicholas Blundell in suit with the King for right of wreck at Ainsdale—Provincial phrases—Nicholas Blundell, M.P. for Lancashire—Feud with the Molyneuxs of Sefton—Award of Cardinal Wolsey in favour of the Blundells—Opposition of the family to the Reformation—Imprisonment of Richard Blundell for harbouring a priest—His death in prison—Forfeitures for recusancy—W. Blundell's narrative of troubles on account of religion — Persecution by Sir Richard Molyneux and Rev. John Nutter, parson of Sefton—Verses on this event—Harkirke burial-ground—Discovery of Saxon coins—W. Blundell prosecuted in Star Chamber and fined heavily.*

THE BLUNDELLS have been seated at Little Crosby, in Lancashire, from very remote times.

B

This village lies near the sea-coast, six miles from
the great maritime town of Liverpool.  At the
present moment the suburbs of this vast town,
soon to be dignified with the title of city, have
stretched out almost to the park walls, and its long
line of docks commences with the newly-constituted
borough of Bootle.  The family is of Norman
descent, and French representatives of the race
are still to be found in good position, using the
original form ' Blondell,' as the name appears in
the roll of Battle Abbey.  Both surnames, Blondell and Blundell, are indeed to be met with in
this famous catalogue, but the former is supposed
to be the more ancient.  The author of the following notes makes mention of a deed, temp[e]
Henry II., in which his ancestor is styled Nicholas
Blondell, but this deed cannot at present be found.
The earliest charter now in possession of the
family is one of that reign, in which John, Earl of
Morton, gives Great Crosby and its appurtenances
to Robert de Ennuylesdale (Ainsdale), his forester,
for homage and service, and a reserved rent of
100 solidi.  This deed is very clearly indited, and
the strong ligature of silk and silver tissue to
which the seal was originally attached is well preserved.  The seal itself has disappeared, and its
loss may perhaps be due to the custom of en-
closing valuable seals in linen bags.  Most of the

seals so covered have crumbled away, whilst others
of an equally early date, to which this attention
has not been paid, are in good preservation.  It is
perhaps worthy of remark that the green wax has
proved more durable than the white, and a friend
who was for many years in the Record Office
declares that his experience in this matter coin-
cides with that of the writer.   The grant above
referred to was confirmed by King John in the
year of his accession to the throne (1199).   Blundell Sands, now the site of numerous villas, and a
portion of the property thus acquired, is still held
by the family ; but the manor and bulk of the
township passed in very early times to the neighbouring family of Molyneux of Sefton.   On the
other hand, the manor and township of Little
Crosby, the present seat of the Blundells, is said
to have been derived from the Molyneuxs.

It is somewhat curious that the first possessions
of the Blundells in this country are intimately
connected with the early fortunes of Liverpool.
In 1208, King John gave Ravinesmols,[1] Annolnes-
dale, &c., to Henry Fitz-Warine of Lancaster
(whose father, Warine, had been the King's fal-
coner), in exchange for Liverpool and Uplither-

---

[1] Raven-meols, formerly a separate lordship, is now included in
Formby.  A large farm still bears the name, which is clearly of
Danish origin, as are Formby, Crosby, &c.

land.[1]   He then ordered his vassals at Toxteth to settle in the new town, and by a grant, dated the same year, constituted it a free burgh.   This was the origin of what is now the most important seaport town in England.   Ainsdale, though under a new feudal lord, remained in the hands of the Blundells, whose representative, Nicholas Blundell, was called upon in 1292 to show why he claimed wreck of the sea on this manor, without the King's licence.   This was at Lancaster, before Hugh de Cressingham and his associates, itinerant judges.

And Nicholas appeared and said that he and all his ancestors from time immemorial had held the said manor, and in like manner had the wreck of the sea all the time, and considered it something annexed and appertaining to the manor ; and had used that liberty up to this time without any interruption of time, and he was prepared to verify this in Court.

And William Inge answered for the King, that in England no one can have or receive wreck but the King and those to whom he concedes the privilege, and as Nicholas the aforesaid can produce no concession of such right from the King or his ancestors, he claims judgment for the King.   More-

---

[1] Up-litherland was likewise for a long period a separate lordship, until absorbed into the township of Aughton.   Here, in a secluded spot, amidst low-lying meadows, stands Walsh Hall, occupying the site of the ancient residence of a branch of the powerful family of Waleys, a name frequently met with in early local charters.

over, it was urged that in point of fact the ancestors of Nicholas had not exercised this liberty *ab antiquo*. [Enquiry is asked.]

The jury declare upon oath that the aforesaid Nicholas had acquired the manor from his father. And they say that Henry, father of the King, gave to the father of Nicholas a certain vessel from a certain wreck which happened in the manor, and no other of the ancestors of Nicholas had ever taken wreck, nor has Nicholas himself, since no wreck has happened. Hence it follows that the King recovers his seisin of the aforesaid wreck when it may happen in the aforesaid manner. [Judgment for the King.][1]

In 1328 Ainsdale was transferred, apparently by marriage settlement, to Gilbert de Halsale, and in 1631 it was purchased from Sir Cuthbert Halsall, along with Birkdale, Meanedale, and Formby, by Robert Blundell of Ince Blundell, Esq., at that period a lawyer of Gray's Inn. It has descended to Thomas Weld Blundell, Esq., and the fortunate position of this property (between Liverpool and Southport) has led to the conversion of a large tract of rabbit warrens into a valuable estate.

Robert de Ainsdale had a son Adam, whose son Robert assumed the name of Blundell, to which family no doubt the grantee of King John belonged. Norman races of distinction were care-

---

[1] Placita de quo Warranto, p. 369.

ful to preserve their patronymics, whilst members
of less distinguished families suffered themselves
to be designated from the properties which they
acquired. Thus, the descendants of William
Gernet became De Lydiates and De Halsalls
from these attained possessions. In the same way
the De Scarisbricks, De Aghtons, De Maghulls
and others are found in this neighbourhood early
in the thirteenth century seated at their respec-
tive manors, while the Molyneuxs and Blundells
alone in these parts retained their ancestral
surnames.

There were several knights amongst the first
Blundells, who were probably all soldiers and
knighted for their prowess in battle. Sir Robert
Blundell accompanied Edward I. in his Welsh
expedition, 1277, and the following year, in view
of eventualities, he made over his estates to his
son Nicholas, reserving to himself 'wreck of the
sea' and certain rents. A curious clause, in
which Nicholas in case of failure in the fulfilment
of the conditions is to pay five marks to the King
for his new work constructing at 'Roye Lane,'
confirms the circumstance of his presence in
Wales, where Edward was then fortifying Rhudd-
lan Castle. The Welsh proved valiant defenders
of their native hills, and it seems probable that
Sir Robert Blundell was one of the fourteen

knights banneret who perished during the absence of the King, in an engagement which was very disastrous to the English arms. The Lion rampant, the present crest of the family, appears on the seal of this interesting deed of Sir Robert Blundell's, whose name encircles the device.

We pass on to notice an early specimen of an English deed, bearing date 1405, which shows the remarkable tenacity of provincial phrases. This document is a declaration of uses by ' Robyn yᵉ Molyneux ' of Melling, in which the same terms are often repeated, so that it affords little scope for variety of phraseology. Still, a few of the expressions used may be worthy of notice. Thus, in the passage, ' Yf he dee bowte hayr of hys bode geyton i weddyd bed yen to,' &c., we find several terms still employed. ' Dee ' for die, ' bowte ' for without, ' geyton ' for begotten, ' i ' for in, ' yen ' then, are frequently heard in this neighbourhood. At the same time it cannot fail to strike the observer, that the number of those who speak the broad vernacular of their forefathers is yearly decreasing. The Fylde country has long been considered the stronghold of Lancashire provincialisms, but even there a notable change is manifest. This change is due not so much to the spread of education, as to the increased facilities of intercommunication leading to a greater refinement of speech, and in some respects of manners.

In 1414 we find Nicholas Blundell of Crosby, one of the knights of the shire for the county of Lancashire, in conjunction with Ralph de Radcliffe, son and heir of Sir Ralph de Radcliffe, Knight, of Smithells and Blackburn. Alice, his daughter, married William Blundell of Ince Blundell, Esq., the representative of the neighbouring branch of this ancient race. It is somewhat curious that this is the only ascertained alliance between the two families. This is the more remarkable as the properties lie contiguous to each other, and both have had resident proprietors for nearly seven centuries, united by the bonds of religion and friendly intercourse. There is no trace of any feud existing between the two houses, at any period of their history, and scarcely even of a passing estrangement on the question of boundaries, that fruitful source of dissension betwixt neighbours.

A century later we meet with a document enumerating the wrongs which Nicholas Blundell, his wife and children, suffered at the hands of Dame Anne Mulnes (Molyneux), and Sir Edward Mulnes, Parson of the Church of Sefton, 'by thare grat myzgth and power.' The Molyneuxs, whose seat was at Sefton, only a short distance from Crosby, had always been a warlike race, and had risen to

eminence by their prowess in the field.  Sir William Molyneux distinguished himself at Agincourt,
and Dame Anne, daughter of Sir John Dutton,
was the widow of his son, Sir Thomas, who died
1491.  Their eldest son, Sir William, in conjunction with Sir William Stanley, led the Lancashire
bowmen at Flodden Field, and contributed greatly
to the success of that memorable engagement.  At
the date of the events recorded in the document
he was absent in the service of his sovereign,
leaving his mother lady paramount at Sefton.  The
allegations of the Blundells show an abuse of power
and a defiance of law on the part of this great
family, which we should hardly have expected to
find in the reign of Henry VIII., although the
' Paston Letters ' have made us familiar with
similar instances of the violence and lawlessness of
powerful nobles at a somewhat earlier date.  The
difference between the parties appears to have
sprung from a disputed claim to certain lands in
Sefton, which the Blundells had possessed from
time immemorial, and for which they were entitled
to receive from the Molyneuxs twenty marks per
annum, which sum the latter refused any longer to
pay.  This land they seized upon, and when the
Blundells endeavoured to regain possession, they
proceeded against them with a high hand, refusing
to abide the award of four ' indifferent ' men, to

whom both parties had agreed to refer the question.  Mr. Blundell declares that they took from
him his right of waifs and strays, and wreck of the
sea, and would not suffer his family to follow
hunting, fishing, and hawking, 'qwech was to yam
grat plesure and tresure.'  They carried off his
tenants at their will, and 'retayned yam to do
yam s'v's in y**ar** time of pleasure.'   Sir Edward
Molyneux, the Parson of Sefton, seems to have
gone the length of practically excommunicating
Mr. Blundell, who complains that he took from him
the right of the Church, and would not suffer him
to 'kneel or tarry' in his chapel on the north side
of Sefton Church.  They broke into his house, spoil-
ing his goods, and carried off a fat ox ; when he
would have defended his premises, they took him
and his son to Lancaster, where they cast them
into prison, and kept them fourteen weeks to his
utter undoing.  They further took possession of a
ward of George Blundell, and parted Nicholas and
his wife, after they had been united three-score
years and had had twelve children together, and
'nev**r** nod**r** cold find fote nod**r** w**t** od**r**,' a picture of
domestic felicity which would have entitled the
couple to the flitch of Dunmow.  In fine, they
drove him out of his house, and kept it by force,
putting in his brother, and they 'occupy his proper
goods moveable and unmoveable.'

This document is in the nature of a petition to the Crown, for redress, and the matter was finally adjudicated upon by Cardinal Wolsey, who in 1526 issued a decree in favour of the Blundells.

At the period of the Reformation the family adhered to the ancient faith, and had much to suffer from the oppressive laws which signalised the latter portion of the reign of Elizabeth. In 1590, Richard Blundell of Crosby was indicted at the Lancaster Assizes, before Judges Church and Walmsley, for having harboured Robert Woodroff, a seminary priest, and being convicted, was committed to prison at Lancaster Castle, along with his son William. A letter to his wife, dated September 28, 1590, has been preserved, in which he speaks of the sickness prevalent within the walls of the prison. He mentions the death of Mr. Worthington of Blainscoe, and the grievous illness of Mr. Latham of Mosborough, both fellow-sufferers in the cause of religion. He himself died there on March 19, 1591–2, the restrictions of confinement and the unwholesomeness of the prison no doubt contributing to hasten his end. William, his son and heir, followed the same course, and, until James I. came to the throne, two-thirds of his lands were in the hands of the Crown for recusancy. He was then able to obtain a royal pardon, and resumed possession of his lands, but after the

Gunpowder Plot, the odium of which fell upon the whole Catholic body, they were again seized by rapacious courtiers, who had begged them from the King. The following statement, written by himself, gives a precise and circumstantial account of the troubles in which he had been involved for conscience' sake :—

In the yeare of our Lord God 1590, the 11th June, the Right Hon<sup>ble</sup> Henrie, Earl of Darbie, sent certaine of his men to searche the house of Richard Blundell of little Crosbie, in the Countie of Lancaster, Esq., for matters belonging to Catholicke Religion, &c., where they apprehended and took away with them to his honor's house (the new Parke) one Mr. Woodroffe, a seminary priest, and the said Richard Blundell, and mee, William Blundell, son of the said Richard : and the day next following we were severally examined by the Earle : and on the thirteenth day of the said month wee were all sent to be imprisoned in Chester Castle. About the 5th or 6th of August next following, wee were all by the Earle's men featched from Chester and brought to Knowesley, one of his honor's houses, where wee were (as alsoe my mother, and one John Carre, my father's man) severally examined by Chatterton the Bishopp of Chester, who was joyned in Comission with the Earle to examine us uppon interrogatories by the Lords of the Councell. And the day following, the priest, my father, and I were sent prisoner to Lancaster (where we found prisoners there before us, Mr. Henrie Latham

of Mosborowe, and Mr. Richard Worthington of
Blainschouge, committed for their conscience),
where also my father and I remained for the most
part until the 19th day of March of the year 1592,
on which day my saide ffather changed this life for
a better. Within about a ffortnight after, I had a
license, obtained from the Right Hon<sup>ble</sup> the Earle
of Derbie, to come to Crosbie for one onely month.
And then returned to Lancaster againe, whence,
about Michælmas ensuing or somewhat before, I
was againe dismissed by his honor's warrant.

And uppon the 20th or 21st November next
after, I was againe apprehended (in the time of
Bell's persecution) by John Nutter, Parson of Sephton, and divers others assisting him, and my wyfe
also was taken, and both of us first weare carried to
the Parsonage of Sephton, and theire staide all
night, whence on the morning wee were brought to
my Lord his house, the New Parke, before the
Earle, the Bishopp Chatterton, and Mr. Wade, one
of the Clearkes of the Councell ; where my wife was
dismissed, and I with others sent to London with
2 Pursevants or Messengers. And on the 8th Decr.
(being the Feast of the Conception of Our bl :
Ladie), I, with an<sup>r</sup> Henrie Latham of Mosborowe,
was by the afforesaid Mr. William Wade brought
before Docter Whyt(gift), Archbishop of Canter-
burie, att his house, Croydon in Surrey, where we
were adjudged to prison, Mr. Latham to the Fleete,
and I to the Gatehouse of Westminster, where I
remained prisoner till the 12th July 1595. Then
was set at libertie uppon bonds to appeare and
come in within 20 dayes after warning given, since

which time I was never imprisoned. And soe
coming home with my wyfe, who had come upp to
London with her brother Edward Norres, and he
returning after a few dayes, she stayed in prison with
mee till my said deliverie, which was some 6 or 8
weeks. And after, we lived at Crosbie untill the
27th May 1598, at what tyme my house was searched
by Sʳ Richard Mollinex, Knt. and John Nutter,
Parson of Sephton, when, I escaping, my wyfe was
taken for her conscience and carried first to Sephton,
and examined, and returned home for that night
uppon bonds or promise of my ffather Norres (as I
thinke) to appeare at Chester before the Bishopp
such a day. Accordingly, the last of the same
month, she, together with other Catholicks, as
namely Hector Stock, Elin Baron, the wyfe of
Laurance Baron of the Edge, Jane Melling, widow,
Elin Blundell, the wyfe of Thomas Blundell of the
Carrside in Ince Blundell, were committed to prison
in the Castle of Chester. And within a little more
than a month after (as I take it), some man (but I
never knew who it was) caused the old indictmᵗ for
entertaineing a Seminary Priest, which had been in
the yeare 1590 afforesaide, to be prosecuted against
me. Whereuppon proclamation was made according to theire custome at the Countie Courts at Lancaster, that I should come in and appeare, which I not
doeing, was condemned of felonie by the Coroner.

After this condemnation I tarried secretly at
countrie houses some 3 quarters of a yeare. And
in the meanwhile my wife, getting out of prison in
Chester Castle uppon bonds for her appearance
againe &c., she and I, for feare of being appre-

hended, went first to Wrixham in Wales, where our
brother Bannister dwelt. And thence after a good
while (my wyfe being great with childe) returned
into Lancashire to the Spekes, and I ridde to Weñie,
where my brother Bannister had another dwelling
house. And thence to London to get a pardon,
where, sending home my horses, I with my man Peter
Stocke staide there about ffive weeks. And, without
getting a pardon, I came into Staffordshire, changing
my name, whither my wyfe came to mee, and theire
we staide about two yeares att six several places
until the Queen's death ; when cominge home, I
soone after obtained from K. James a free and
large pardon, which cost me in all but either 40 or
50 shillings.

He also gives a list of all those who begged
his lands from the Crown, and the result, but this
document is too long for insertion here.

In connection with the long imprisonment of
Mrs. Blundell at Chester, mentioned in the fore-
going narrative, a curious letter is extant at Crosby,
dated August 23, 1598, which bears the signature
of Sir Richard Molyneux, Knt., and Rev. John
Nutter, Parson of Sefton, the ' Golden Ass ' of
Queen Elizabeth. This is an application to the
Bishop of Chester on behalf of Mrs. Blundell, whose
release they ask for on the ground of ill health.
One very suggestive passage may be noticed :—

And for that common experience doth too well
teach us that yᵉ evill examples of such Archpapists

and disobedient persons doe greatlie hinder the race of yᵉ Gospell (especiallie in these maritime parts) and daylie threaten dangerous events, if yᵉ same be not wislie foreseene and speedilie prevented : wee could wish oʳ selves likewise altogether freede from the company of Mr. Blundell if by any lawful way or meanes he (being a confyned Papist) might be removed from among us.

It is not clear whether the death of Mr. Blundell or only his banishment is here hinted at.

This staunch recusant has left behind him in manuscript several treatises on controversial matters, and many poems of a religious character. One of the latter consisting of seventeen stanzas was written, as he states, at the time of the above persecution. He appears to have wooed the muses with little success, but we give the following stanza of this poem, not for the sake of its versification, but to show what sort of trials those had to endure, who in this country, three centuries ago, refused to accept the new ordinances in matters of religion, which were then being forced upon the nation :—

Husbands and their wives parted are asunder,
Parents severed are from their children dear.
Sucking babes do cry
Which at home do lie ;
Mothers do bewayle
Being fast in gaol ;
All the country talketh
Every way one walketh,

What in Sefton we endure
For no strange opinion
But that old religion
Austin planted here most sure.

In 1611, Mr. Blundell, finding his fellow Catholics refused burial at their Parish Church (Sefton), ordered a plot within his own grounds to be set apart for this purpose. The place selected was called Harkirke—the hoary or ancient church—and the tradition that a church had once existed there probably influenced his choice. In preparing the ground many scores of Saxon coins were discovered, chiefly of the reign of Alfred the Great; and Mr. Blundell caused a copper-plate to be engraved in which thirty-two of these coins are represented. This plate has been preserved at Crosby, as well as a description of the coins written by himself; but not altogether correct: the coins themselves have disappeared. Later on, this act of humanity, coming to the knowledge of Government, was the occasion of a severe sentence being pronounced against him. For when the Sheriff and his followers, in attempting a levy upon his goods for recusancy, had met with some resistance on the part of his tenants, he was summoned before that all-potent tribunal, the Star Chamber. This happened in the year 1629, and the result is thus given in Rushworth's 'Historical Collections,' vol. ii. p. 21 :—

And y^e defendant Blundell being a Popish Recusant convict, and living in Little Crosby in Lancashire, enclosed a piece of ground and fenced it, part with a stone wall and part with a hedge and ditch, and kept and used the same for the space of 10 years for the burial of Popish Recusants and Seminary Priests, and for these offences 2 of the rioters were fined 500*l.* a piece and 3 others 100*l.* a piece, and Blundell for procurement of the riots and erecting the Churchyard, 2,000*l.* All committed to y^e Fleet, and the walls and mounds of the Church-yard to be pulled down by the Sheriff, and y^e ground laid waste, by decree to be read at y^e assizes.

From further documents it appears that the fine was afterwards reduced to 500*l.* The sum of 80*l.* was awarded to the Sheriff, Sir Ralph Ashton, whose acknowledgment to Mr. Blundell for the payment of this amount on July 20, 1629, is now before the writer.

This stout sufferer for conscience sake died at Crosby, at the age of 78, on July 2, 1638, and was succeeded in his estates by his grandson William, the author of the following notes.

## CHAPTER II.

### WILLIAM BLUNDELL THE CAVALIER.

*Birth at Crosby—Secret Jesuit Schools in England—Early Marriage at Haggerston—Becomes Captain of Dragoons —Commission signed by Sir Thomas Tildesley—Lamed at Lancaster—Sufferings in the Civil Wars—Fourth Imprisonment at Liverpool—Statement of his Losses—Sequestration of his Estate for Ten Years—Purchases it with Borrowed Money—Enormous Bill of Fines for Arrears of Recusancy—Goes Abroad—At Breda with King Charles II.—Accompanies him to Dover—Fresh Persecutions—Titus Oates' Plot—His friend Richard Langhorne one of its victims—Letters on the Plot—His Son Nicholas accused by Oates—Correspondence with Sir Roger l'Estrange.*

WILLIAM BLUNDELL the Cavalier was born at Crosby Hall on July 15, 1620, and lost his father Nicholas in 1631, when he was but eleven years of age. His mother, Jane, daughter of Roger Bradshaigh, Esq. of Haigh, near Wigan, survived till August 26, 1640. It seems probable that he received his early instruction from his father or grandfather, and was afterwards sent to one of the secret places of education well known to those who adhered to the ancient faith. That there were several such in various parts of the kingdom, is evident from the frequent reference made to them in the reports of the Government spies and informers. In 1635 a draft warrant was issued by the Privy Council for the search of Stanley Grange, the residence of the Hon. Anne Vaux, where the Jesuit Fathers had established a school. In this case, timely notice of the intended visit having been received, the school was found to be broken up and the boys dispersed. A more successful raid on Mr. Levison's house, near Wolverhampton, resulted in the capture of several youths, who were in the end restored to their parents. It does not appear that Mr. Blundell was trained at St. Omer's College, for though he speaks favourably of the system of education pursued at that famous Jesuit Seminary, yet he expressly says that he derived this opinion from the fruits of learning and virtue which he perceived in others. Moreover, the circumstance of his never having acquired the French language until late in life sufficiently proves that he never resided in a foreign seminary. In fact, the period allowed him for education was too short for him to have spent his time abroad, for he was summoned to take an active part in life at an unusually early age. But whoever taught him did the work well, securing for his pupil a solid founda-

tion of learning and a love of letters which he
never lost. In consequence of the death of his
eldest son and heir, the grandfather was anxious
to make a fresh settlement of his estates during
his own lifetime. This was of particular impor-
tance in the case of recusants, as two-thirds of
their landed property lay at the mercy of the
crown, and hence it was very desirable that the
holder should only possess a life interest in the
estate. This rendered necessary the early marriage
of William Blundell, who, when but fifteen, es-
poused Ann, daughter of Sir Thomas Haggerston,
of Haggerston, co. Northumberland, Bart. In
one of his letters to Lady Haggerston, written in
1651, there is an interesting reference to his youthful and martial appearance when he came as a
suitor to the fair Northumbrian home, from which
he drew his partner in the joys and sorrows of a
long career :—

> I remember there was a young fellow not far
> from Haggerston, that told a friend of ours that
> would gladly have drawn him to the wars, that it
> was a great pity 'so gude a like man as he should
> be knocked o'th head.' You will remember what a
> pretty, straight young thing, all dashing in scarlet, I
> came to Haggerston, &c.

The dashing scarlet attire must have added to
the attraction of his youthful figure, and such an

apparition would have found favour at other places
besides Haggerston.   If he could not entice a
sturdy yeoman to the field, another voice answered
more readily to his call.   His wife happily proved
all that he had hoped for, and in 1665, writing to
the same lady, he alludes to her thus pleasantly :—

> And now, when I speak of your ark, I must
> here acknowledge that the dove which was sent
> from thence, some thirty years ago, hath saved from
> sinking our little cock-boat at Crosby in many a
> storm.

In the early part of his wedded career, Mr.
Blundell led a life of gaiety, and readily gave himself to the pursuit of pleasure with little thought
of the morrow.   He afterwards bitterly lamented
his great and continual charge at this time in
horses, dogs, hawks, play, apparel, and a thousand
other excesses.   A few lively poetical pieces written
at this period evince the delight he took in plays,
dances, and other country amusements.   He visited
Dublin in 1638, and was entertained at the court
of the unfortunate Earl of Strafford, then at the
height of his short-lived glory.   He describes the
almost regal state assumed by the Lord Deputy,
the first nobleman of Ireland, the Marquis (afterwards Duke) of Ormond being amongst his re-
tainers.   In these pursuits, without the aid of more
destructive sources of expenditure, he was gradually

involving himself in debt, when he was called to a sense of his duty and to more serious occupations by the summons of war. The King was rallying his adherents round his standard, and had gratefully responded to the applications of certain loyal Lancashire Catholics to be permitted to take up arms in his defence. With all the ardour of youth Mr. Blundell threw himself into the struggle, accepting a captain's commission from Sir Thomas Tildesley, Knt., authorising him to raise a company of 100 dragoons for the royal cause. This commission, dated **Leigh, December 22, 1642,** bearing the neat signature of the famous Lancashire General, is still preserved at Crosby, and is couched in the following terms :—

By virtue of his Ma^{ts} commission under his signe manuall to mee directed, I doe hereby constitute and appointe yo^u William Blundell Esq^re to bee Captaine of one companie of Dragoones in my Regiment. And I doe hereby give yo^u full power and authoritie for his Ma^{tie} and his name to raise, impresse and retaine the said companie, raised or to bee raised by sound of Drumme or anie other waie (and in anie of his Ma^{ts} Dominions) for the defence of his Ma^{ts} royall person, the 2 houses of Parliament, the Protestant religion, the lawe of the land, the libertie and propertie of the subject and Priveledge of Parliament, and when soe raised to bringe together and employ in his Ma^{ts} service as you shall from tyme to tyme receive directions for.

And I doe hereby require all the inferiour officers and souldiers of y^e companie yo^u to obey as their Capitane, yo^u likewise obeying your superiour officers according to the discipline of warre.[1]

The quota was still incomplete, when Mr. Blundell was called upon to join Lord Strange in the neighbourhood of Preston. The latter nobleman, by the death of his father, had become Earl of Derby before the march to Lancaster was undertaken. A work by Madam Guizot de Witt, entitled 'The Lady of Latham,' which contains several particulars derived from family documents, gives the following account of this expedition :—

Lord Derby left Latham House on 17th March (1642–3) after nightfall, and after a forced march of about 30 miles, the little army appeared the next morning before the walls of Lancaster. The garrison were summoned to surrender, and indignantly refused ; the soldiers hesitated to make a second attack, when the Earl of Derby, seizing a short

[1] A reduced facsimile of this Commission is given as a frontispiece ; it is taken with permission from a full-size impression which accompanies two papers by the editor, entitled 'A Century of Recusancy,' read before the Historic Society of Lancashire and Cheshire, and printed with the proceedings for 1879. In these papers a few of the documents and letters here given are made use of, with several additional ones having reference to that particular subject. It may likewise be here mentioned, that four articles from the same pen were inserted in the *Month* (October 1878, to January 1879), under the title of 'A Loyal Catholic Cavalier.' In these will be found some specimens of the following notes, and of the numerous letters of Mr. Blundell.

pike, sprang forward, crying, 'Follow me.' Some gentlemen volunteers immediately joined him, and urged the soldiers on. The assault was made, the city taken, and the fortifications raised.'

Mr. Blundell was one of those who responded with alacrity to the call of their leader. The gallantry of this little band exposed it to the severe fire of the garrison, and he received a serious wound, having his thigh shattered with a musket-shot. Seacome—of whom Dr. Ormerod, the historian of Cheshire, remarks that, though untrustworthy in other matters, he may be relied on in what relates to the civil war—in describing this engagement, says, ' Mr. Blundell, that gallant, loyal, and worthy gentleman, was wounded on entering the city.' He was carried to Dinkley, the residence of Colonel Talbot, then engaged on the King's side, where every attention was paid him. In after years, writing to Mrs. Talbot, he recalls his obligations to her, reminding her of the long week which he spent in her hospitable mansion, where he was nursed with so much tenderness in his sore infirmity. This wound had the effect of rendering him a cripple for life, and in his own neighbourhood, his tenants, indulging the Lancashire propensity for nicknames, commonly called him, ' Halt-Will.' He himself tells us that he had to wear a very high-heeled shoe, and calculated that he had

E

lost three inches in height by reason of his accident. From this period till the close of the civil war, his life was one of privation and anxiety. He resided during these disastrous years chiefly in the houses of friends and acquaintance, his constant good humour making him a general favourite. As he was in continual danger of being taken prisoner, he was compelled to leave his own house at Crosby to the care of his wife, or of his sister Frances, a woman of rare courage and prudence. So exposed were they, while the war lasted, to domiciliary visits, in which the soldiers carried off anything they could lay their hands upon, that they were obliged to bury their bread from meal to meal. One advantage which Mr. Blundell undoubtedly drew from his misfortunes, was the conviction that they were sent him as a wholesome correction, to withdraw him from the vain pursuit of pleasure, and to fix his mind on more lasting possessions. This is evident from numberless letters and remarks, some of which will be found in the following pages. 'Periissem nisi periissem,' was the motto to which he clung in after life, for he declares that he would have been lost, as regards his fortunes both here and hereafter, if it had not been for this merciful visitation.

Being totally disabled from all active employment, he could do little to aid his party, and must have watched the waning cause of the Royalists with dismay. A letter of his to a friend in the Isle of Man sends intelligence which he desires may be communicated to the Earl of Derby. He was thrice imprisoned at this period, and again a fourth time, in 1657, at Liverpool, which he describes as a loathsome prison. From a letter dated March 17, 1657–8, it appears that his confinement had then lasted ten weeks. This was probably in some part of the Castle, which had been dismantled during the civil war. Here he had for a companion his uncle, Christopher Bradshaigh, and the Hon. Richard Butler, heir to the title and impaired fortunes of Viscount Mountgarret. When this young man was released, after a long imprisonment, his uncle, Colonel Mervin Touchet, requested Mr. Blundell to receive him for a time at his house at Crosby. There he remained for two years, his father and friends being unwilling, perhaps unable, to assist him with the means necessary for his return to Ireland. It is not surprising that, under these circumstances, he formed an attachment to Emilia, Mr. Blundell's eldest daughter. This resulted in a marriage in 1661, but the young couple had many privations to endure, until their accession to the title in 1679. The Duke of Ormond, the head of the house of Butler, proved a warm friend, and for many years

they resided at Kilkenny, near the mansion of
their noble benefactor. From this couple, the present Henry Edmund, thirteenth Viscount Mountgarret, descends.

By the law of 1646, no Papist delinquent could
compound for his estate ; consequently, all Mr.
Blundell's estate was seized and remained in the
hands of the Commissioners for nine or ten years.
His trials at this period, in the loss of goods and
the ravages committed upon his lands, were very
severe. The following is a record preserved in his
handwriting :—

> The war between Charles I. and his Parliament
> began A.D. 1642. That year, March 18, my thigh
> was broken with a shot in the King's service. A.D.
> 1643, all my goods and most of my lands were
> sequestered for being a Papist and delinquent, as
> the prevailing party call the King's partakers. In
> the year 1645, my wife farmed my demesne at
> Crosby, and all her quick goods being lost, she
> bought one horse and two oxen to make up a team.
> A.D. 1646, November 13, I valued all my goods,
> and comparing them with my debts, I found myself
> worse than nothing by the whole sum of 81*l.* 18*s.*,
> my lands being all lost. A.D. 1653 : Till this year,
> from 1646 inclusively, I remained under sequestra-
> tion, having one-fifth part allowed to my wife, and
> farming only from the sequestrators my demesne of
> Crosby and the mill. About Midsummer 1653, my
> whole estate was purchased and compounded for

with my own money, for my use, so that in the month of February 1653-4, I was indebted 1,100*l.* 7*s.*, after which time I was so overcharged with care, debts, business, and imprisonments, that I think I took no account of the value of my goods till the year 1658.

In the repurchase of his estate, Mr. Blundell employed the intervention of two Protestant friends—his cousin, Sir Roger Bradshaigh, Bart., of Haigh, and Mr. Gilbert Crouch. The sum paid appears to have been 1,340*l.*, representing, no doubt, his life interest in the property. In addition to this Mr. Blundell found himself saddled with the arrears of rents reserved to the Crown, arising out of frequent grants for recusancy, some of which had never been discharged. These went as far back as the reign of Elizabeth, and though Mr. Blundell represented the injustice of charging him with rents which should have been paid by those who had the benefit of the forfeitures, the Government was inexorable, and he was compelled to pay on this score 1,167*l.* 15*s.* 6½*d.* Moreover, the cost of making out this prodigious bill was added to the account, making an addition of 34*l.* 10*s.* 2*d.* to the foregoing sum. This remarkable document, a roll of twenty feet in length, has been carefully preserved at Crosby. May it long serve to remind his descendants of the faith and loyalty of their ancestor.

In 1658, Mr. Blundell procured a pass from Colonel Gilbert Ireland to go abroad, which he made use of to conduct two of his daughters to Rouen, where they were desirous of embracing a religious life. An incidental reference to the journey, which he makes in a letter written subsequently to these daughters, reveals some of the inconveniences to which travellers were subjected at that period.

> When you went from my poor house to Rouen, part of your journey was on horseback, some little part on foot, the most by coach, and the rest in a tottering bark or cockboat upon the unstable element of water, not without crosswinds and perhaps a tempest. Besides these you may remember some other varieties in that journey, as our stop at Liverpool water, the brawls, the lets, and other accidents in the coach and in the inns ; and at the last, when we came to London, the unexpected death of the greatest person (Oliver Cromwell), as we esteemed him, upon the whole earth, was the occasion, by shutting up of the sea-ports, of a notable stop in your journey.

Our Cavalier was still abroad in 1660, when England was preparing to welcome again her legitimate monarch. Attracted by the gathering of royalists at Breda, he hastened thither and had an interview with Charles the night before his embarkation. He renewed on this occasion to his

King the offer of his fortunes and life, and no doubt heard him utter those promises of toleration which were so soon forgotten. He accompanied him in the same ship to Dover, where he was a witness of the joy and acclamations which greeted his arrival. An interesting anecdote, recorded in the following pages, in which we find King Charles measuring his height against the lintel of the cabin door, shows that the King was of more than ordinary stature. None of his followers could attain the measure of royalty ; but perhaps the tallest practised a wise abstention, qualifying themselves thus early for the *rôle* of courtiers.

Whatever benefits some of the party may have derived from the Restoration, those of an obnoxious faith had little to expect. At first there was a gleam of sunshine and a certain degree of relaxation from the severities of the penal laws ; but soon the Anti-Popery cry was renewed, and persecution became the order of the day. The King's easy nature induced him to accede to fresh measures of repression, and the report of the conversion of the Duke of York was not calculated to alter the temper of the nation. At length the audacious plot concocted by Titus Oates found the country ready to listen to any extravagance, and worked it into the frenzy of a religious panic. The voice of justice and reason was no longer heard, and many innocent Catholics, both priests and laymen, became the victims of popular fury.

Among the sufferers was Richard Langhorne, Esq., a lawyer of eminence and a consistent Catholic, with whom Mr. Blundell had long before contracted what he styles, in the language of the day, 'an entire friendship.' Many letters had passed between them, and in 1666 Mr. Langhorne sent his friend an interesting account of the Great Fire of London, of which he was an eye-witness. A remarkable letter, bearing date May 14, 1673, written by Mr. Blundell, we cannot forbear quoting in part. It reveals the consternation with which Catholics beheld the signs of the times, and their apprehension of what was to follow. It will be seen that Mr. Blundell echoes a sentiment of his correspondent, which, taken in connection with his subsequent fate, seems couched in the language of prophecy. It is clear also that Mr. Blundell would have been equally ready to suffer death in the same cause.

You think we are all asleep, and that we shall be 'eating and drinking, marrying and giving in marriage,' when the storm and the flood come. Shall I tell you my fancy? Perhaps you will say it is a wild one. I think that none but madmen can execute those cruel things that are threatened against His Majesty's Catholic subjects. And if men be really mad, there is no defence against them by paper walls. In my younger days our next Justice of the Peace (Colonel Moore, of Bank Hall) sent one of my tenants, a soldier of the trained bands, to the gaol for refusing the oath of allegiance. He was prisoner a year or two, and being at last released in time of the war, he took up arms for the King, and lived and died (with his poor estate sequestered) a loyal Catholic subject ; whilst that very same Justice of the Peace was one of the King's Judges and died (for aught I know) an unrepenting rebel. I knew no leading rebel about those times who was not, as I confidently think, a notable taker or tenderer of the oath of allegiance, nor any one Catholic refuser who proved disloyal to his King. God grant us a better test of allegiance, a more lucky oath.

I have a villainous book of Prynne's printed in 1643, where he endeavours to prove by the records of sundry kingdoms, that the people had authority to depose and resist their kings, to call them to strict account, and, when they saw just cause for it, to proceed capitally against them. According to these same grounds, King Charles I. was beheaded. When the bloody deed was done, Milton and sundry others by writing, and thousands of others by the sword, defended it as just. Yet Milton and those are pardoned and live in security. Prynne, as is very well known, was an eminent Parliament man, a mortal foe to the Papists, and was cherished with a very fair salary and with singular places of trust since the King came in. I think we do not seek for preferment. For my own part, I

F

am sure I only plead 'pro domo mea,' for the same house and lands which I lost for my duty to the King, to a pack of those arch villains, and purchased it from them again after 9 or 10 years' sequestration, with money which I borrowed. My limbs, my goods, my liberty, I lost on the same account. Many others of ours lost life and all. And ours and our greatest enemies' principles are still the same. If we must therefore beg or hang, I pray God bless the King, and the will of God be done. My dearest sir, I wish as much as you that *we were together one day before we suffer*, and I shall not despair of this happiness, neither will I be cross or wilful in refusing advice, &c.

In a letter to the same gentleman, dated February 22, 1677, Mr. Blundell speaks of the fresh exactions in his neighbourhood, to which the revival of the persecution had given rise.

.   .   .  Many seizures have here (in these parts) been made of y$^e$ estates of convicted Recusants. If y$^e$ Inquisitions had not been indifferently favorable, they had been utterly ruined. Y$^e$ Papists, I presume, do take it a little unkindly, after an 18 years' sequestration suffered under y$^e$ usurpers, to be sequestered again by y$^a$ King, and to be jeered no doubt for theire loyalty by y$^e$ old oppressors. Here is one of my poore neighbours hardly put too't by many expenceful shifts to keepe off for a tyme a judgement and y$^e$ execution necessarily following, upon a verdict given against him about 18 months agoe by force of y$^e$ statute for 20*l.* a month for his absence from church service. For my own part, you know I am wholly for liberty of conscience ; yet would I have them humbly to submit their fortunes to the secular power. . . .

In a letter to Lady Bradshaigh dated December 26, 1678, he writes :

Notwithstanding the great disloyalty of very many persons (as it seems) who had lived in good repute, I cannot accuse myself of any such crime. And although by confinement, disarming and other waies I may appear to be one of y$^e$ wicked, yet, for as much as concerns either my allegiance to y$^e$ King, or my hearty true respects to my worthy friends, I defy y$^e$ whole world and y$^e$ Devil himself to prove it.

Another letter relating to this eventful period, and dated April 4, 1679, is addressed to Mr. John North, of Dublin. It is valuable, as expressing the personal sentiments of Mr. Blundell on a matter regarding which the religion of Catholics has often exposed them to the suspicion of disloyalty. But neither the past sufferings of our Cavalier on behalf of the Crown, nor his present protestations, could avail him as long as he adhered to the proscribed creed of his forefathers.

I have been inwardly no little afflicted to see and hear those many astonishing particulars w$^{ch}$ have filled y$^e$ world with wonder, and to be constrained either to believe that many of those very same persons, who being of my own profession had once been active assertors of y^e Royal cause and painful sufferers for it, have since contrived y^e worst of treasons against it ; or else to believe or think . . . that there hath been an unchristian confederacy against ye reputation, lives and fortunes of many innocent men. I was troubled a little som months agoe to see my trusty old sword taken frō me (w^ch had been my companion w^n I lost my limbs, my lands, my liberty for acting against the rebels in the King's behalf) by an officer appointed for y^e purpose, who in that former old war had been a captaine against y^e King. Yet I hear no personal charge against me, nor do I fear any at all, saving purely upon y^e account of y^e religion w^ch I have ever profest. In that particular I conceive that my estate and my liberty, as well as many others, may incur no little damage, if y^e Parlements will be done ; and if that be y^e King's will too, I shall most heartily and humbly submit. I have formerly suffered the loss of a fair personal estate and sequestration of all my lands for 10 long years and upwards. After w^ch I bought y^e same lands off y^e rebels in y^e year 53 with y^e money w^ch I borrowed off my friends. I was 4 tymes taken prisoner and p^d my ransom twice. All this was for my loyalty to y^e King. I deny, as in y^e presence of God, y^t I have ever entertained any designe w^tsoever contrary to y^e duty of a subject eyther against that K. or this. And as for invasions, it hath ever been my professed principle, that all even Catholic subjects of a lawful Protestant king (such as King Charles y^e 2^d) are obliged faithfully to adhere to that King in all invasions w$^t$soever, though made by Catholic princes or even by the Pope himself.

Mr. Langhorne suffered resolutely on July 14, 1679, asserting in his last speech that he had an offer of a free pardon if he would have renounced his religion. The judge who condemned him (Justice Scroggs) afterwards declared that he was convinced of his innocence, for which he was taken to task by Oates and Bedloe. This must have been a very anxious time for Mr. Blundell, as, in addition to his friend's prosecution, his own son Nicholas had been marked out as one of the victims for destruction. He had entered the Society of Jesus in 1662, and was arrested at Lambeth by the pursuivants of Oates, who declared that he had revealed to him the plan for the burning of London. He must have been speedily released from custody, and was present at the trial of the accused, of which he gives many particulars in a letter to a nun at Cambray, which has found its way into the State Archives at Brussels. Extracts from the letter may be seen in the ample account of this conspiracy, contained in the fifth volume of Foley's 'Records of the English Province,' S. J. This work, of which the last volume has only recently appeared, is not sufficiently known. It embodies more original information respecting the Catholic body during the operation of the penal laws than any work hitherto published.

Another of Mr. Blundell's correspondents was the well-known political writer Roger l'Estrange, Esq. (afterwards knighted), who published an ' Intelligencer,' which his friend was able to join a neighbour in procuring twice a week. From some passages in his letters, it is probable that he furnished occasional items of news for this journal. Mr. Blundell seems to have had some difficulty in getting his correspondent to put the right address upon his letters. Thus on June 1, 1664, he says in a postscript :

> If you do ever remember me again, I pray forget not Liverpool, for your two last letters being directed to Preston (20 miles off) came late to my hand. Liverpool is 5 from hence and even from thence the passage to us dependeth very often upon the market day.

Writing the following month from ' Westchester,' he says :

> Yours of the 2d, directed to Crosby in Cheshire, I have caught to day in my journey to Chester. You shot 6 bows over Crosby when you aimed at Preston, and now at Cheshire you are three or four short. Surely I shall take myself for some great body, for every shaft will hit me though shot at random.

## CHAPTER III.

WILLIAM BLUNDELL THE CAVALIER—*continued.*

*Mr. Blundell's Activity—Hunting—His friend Laurence
Ireland, of Lydiate, becomes a Jesuit—Bills of Mortality
—Bowling at Sefton—Prevalence of Drink—Duelling—
Remarkable Answer to an expected Challenge — The
Moores of Bank Hall—Intended Banishment of Ca-
tholics—List of the Proscribed in Lancashire—Difficulty
in obtaining a Pass—Abroad at La Fleche—Draws up
Petition to James II.—Suggests Plan for Defeat of
Cavalry—Fifth Imprisonment at Manchester—Discharge
and Five-miles Chain—Patriotic Grant to a Seaman—
His Son William carried off Prisoner for Lancashire
Plot—Death of the Cavalier—Petition to the Crown—
Little Crosby Village.*

NOTWITHSTANDING his lameness, Mr. Blundell's
activity, both of mind and body, was very great.
He visited, as may be seen from the following
notes, many places of interest at home and abroad,
concerning which he has several curious notices.
His hurt does not seem to have prevented him
from riding, or from following the diversion of
hunting, of which he was particularly fond.  His
cousin, Sir Roger Bradshaigh of Haigh, kept a
pack of hounds, as also did his kinsman and

neighbour, Laurence Ireland, of Lydiate, Esq. He
carefully records the bugle notes of Sir Roger's
huntsman, also his 'recheat' or recall of the hunting party. He gives also the 'recheat' (a much
longer one) of his friend Mr. Ireland. This gentleman, the last of the Lydiate branch of the Irelands
of Hutte and Hale, when a widower at the age of
thirty-one, having settled his estates on his elder
daughter Margaret (afterwards married to Sir
Charles Anderton, Second Baronet of Lostock),
left the world and became a Jesuit and a priest.
Mr. Blundell, in his letters to his friend and to Sir
Thomas Preston, of the Manor, Furness, Bart.,
who some time afterwards, under similar circumstances, entered the same Society, seems to envy
their lot, and tells them that they have chosen the
better part. He reminds Laurence Ireland of the
last house but one at which they had met to join a
hunting party. On this occasion his friend remarked to him that whenever he heard the triple
note of the bugle sounding to the chase, it seemed
to cry out to him 'Dead, Dead, Dead.' Whilst
abroad, Mr. Blundell furnished him, at his request,
with what he calls 'bills of mortality.' Three or
four of these very interesting communications have
been copied into his letter-book, and they contain,
besides much local news, many matters of general
interest. In a letter dated 1668 occurs this passage:

The noble Countess of Southampton hath been here four or five weeks amongst us, bowling on Sephton Green ; the country came flowing in, and she kept a public table at the Hall of Maile (Maghull). I could have soured her cheer by giving her bills of mortality since the last scene she acted in this neighbourhood. But I was so sour myself, that I saw not so much as a brace of rubbers on the Green during the whole play. *Quantum mutatus.*

It must be presumed that the once fashionable pastime alluded to was the attraction which drew Barbara Villiers, Duchess of Cleveland and Countess of Southampton, one of the numerous mistresses of Charles II., from the fascinations of a Court to so remote a spot as Maghull. From a letter written about this time by the Cavalier's son William to his brother-in-law, Lawrence, son of Rowland Eyre of Hassop, co. Derbyshire, Esq., it would appear that a bowling club had been established at Sefton under distinguished auspices :

If you could have time to make a step into Lancashire, I would show you once a week a meeting of a dozen or fourteen gentlemen, or more, who, after a dinner had at Sefton, spend the afternoon at bowls. My Lord Molineux and his son (who is lately come out of Italy), Sir Edward Stanley, my cousin Scarisbrick, and others have engaged to meet at Sefton every week. Sir Edward Stanley has set afoot bows and arrows, and follows the sport very eagerly. My Lord Molineux his son intends to do the like. So that you will find other diversion besides downright drinking.

From the last expression it may be inferred that the praiseworthy encouragement given to these innocent recreations by the heads of the chief families in this part, was with the view of counteracting that evil. That it was a great evil at that period, is evident from Mr. Blundell's correspondence.

In his bills of mortality the number of deaths amongst the gentry, which he attributes to what he calls 'the vice of our country,' is very large. He mentions the appalling circumstance of a 'notable observing youth' having reckoned no fewer than fifty burials of rich and poor within the space of one year in Prescot parish alone, all caused by immoderate drinking. This shows the prevalence of this vice to an alarming extent, fostered as it was by the example of the higher orders. Mr. Blundell gives more than one example of a young man challenged and shot dead by his host, who chose to think himself insulted when his guest refused his cups. Whatever may be the case at present with regard to the lower orders, it is certain that there is a manifest improvement amongst those of the higher class, since the days of deep drinking have gone out.

In the following notes frequent reference will

be found to the subject of duelling, another prevalent vice of the times. Mr. Blundell's mind
seems to have been much exercised by this question ; but he was clearly of opinion that it was
unlawful either to give or to accept a challenge.
He says that a man whose courage has been
proved can refuse a challenge without imputation
of cowardice, and he brings an example to show
how a man should act whose valour has not been
put to the test. How Mr. Blundell himself would
have acted in such a case, is evident from the
following remarkable answer which he had prepared in anticipation of a challenge. Here we
find the noblest sentiments of a Christian and the
exalted courage of a cavalier happily blended :

> I have lost much blood in defence of the laws,
> and will not hazard any to break them. I confess I
> dare not be damned upon any account, and am
> unwilling to be hanged upon this. I have not learnt
> the ways to evade the hand of justice when I am
> guilty of blood. In short, I will neither meet you
> nor any man, how strong or weak he may be, with
> so bad a design, and I propose, by God's assistance,
> that the most public or great affront that malice
> shall devise against me, shall not move me from
> this resolution. If I have done wrong to you or
> any man else, I will hazard my blood and fortune
> (in a just and honourable way) so far to make
> amends ; and in this I shall always be willing to
> submit to indifferent judges. In the mean time,

if this answer displeases you, I shall never decline
the walks to which my business leads me out of any
fear of your sword, &c.

Mr. Blundell says that the party from whom
he had good reason to expect a challenge was a
person of great repute, and from another passage
we gather that it was Colonel Moore, his neighbour of Bank Hall.   This gentleman was the only
Protestant magistrate in the neighbourhood, and
had given much annoyance to him and his tenants
on the score of religion.   Mr. Blundell had written
some verses concerning him which were not of a
complimentary character, and possibly had expressed his sentiments in language which would
be called in these days ' unparliamentary.'   As
Colonel Moore died in Dublin about 1650, having
accompanied Cromwell to Ireland at the head of
a force, this answer must have been written before
that period.   He was one of the members of Parliament whose names we find appended to the
warrant for the execution of Charles I.   Notwithstanding the injuries received from the family, Mr.
Blundell, on occasion of an epidemic (said to have
been small-pox), when Mrs. Moore had her husband (Edward, afterwards Sir Edward Moore,
Baronet, son of the Colonel) sick and three children dead in the house, went no less than four
times to visit and console her.   At this time none

of her friends would come near the place, and it is a curious sign of the credulity of the age, that Mrs. Moore could not be persuaded that her children had succumbed to any natural distemper, but ascribed their death to witchcraft.

So great was the excitement produced throughout the country by the accusations of Titus Oates, that besides the exclusion of the Catholic Peers from the House of Lords, which was effected in 1678, the banishment of all the leading Catholics of the kingdom was seriously contemplated. This was perhaps found to be too severe and impolitic a measure to be carried out. Lists of the intended victims were prepared in 1680 by the aid of the returns of the names of recusants made at that time. Sir Roger Bradshaigh sent Mr. Blundell a catalogue of Popish recusants of the greatest quality in Lancashire, whom it was proposed to banish. This he had procured from the Earl of Ancram, and we find Caryll Viscount Molyneux at the head of the list, which comprises sixty-four names, including those of Mr. Blundell and his son William. He had previously applied to Government for a pass to go abroad, and was informed that he could not have one, unless he entered into recognisances not to return into England without a licence. Mr. Blundell indignantly refused a permission coupled with so hard a condition,

and thus expresses himself in a letter to Lord
Ancram :—

> 22 Aug. 1679. . . . I have engaged in 500*l.*
> already not to travel to Rome, and now to banish
> myself by a deliberate act of my own from my
> native and best beloved country, I have not the
> heart to do. I should certainly forfeit my bond if
> nothing else would effect my return. I would rather
> be confined again (as once in the prime of my youth
> for the noblest cause in the world) to my plundered
> bare walls and a pair of crutches, than to lead the
> life of an outlaw. I desire, as the case now stands,
> rather to keep my possession till the law of the land
> or of nature do turn me out.

Later on he procured a licence free from the
obnoxious condition, and passed over into France,
where he spent a good part of the following year.
He resided chiefly at La Fleche, for the sake of his
grandson the Honourable Edmund Butler, who was
then pursuing his studies at the Jesuit Academy.

During the short reign of James II. our Cavalier was frequently in London, where he had many
friends at Court, who encouraged him with the
hope of at length obtaining some compensation
for his many trials. At their suggestion he prepared a petition to the King, and was led to expect that he might receive some post, though, as
he himself says, he hardly knew what sort of an
office would suit a man of his years and infirmities.

This petition, which is inserted at the conclusion of this sketch, does not appear to have been actually presented, and the end of his hopes and those of his friends came very speedily. When the news of the Prince of Orange's intended landing reached England, the martial instincts of the old cavalier were aroused, and he addressed a letter to the Honourable Robert Strickland, Vice-Chamberlain to the Queen, suggesting a plan for the discomfiture of the enemy's troop of horse, which was said to be incomparably strong. This plan was the planting of a number of sharp-pointed rods (tipped with iron, if possible) to be so placed as to impale the horses of the troopers when they rushed to the attack. He goes into details, describing, with the precision of a quartermaster, the size of the rods, the quantity required, and the wagons desirable for their transportation. Whatever military men may think of this scheme, to a non-combatant it wears rather an impracticable appearance, as its success seems wholly to depend upon the enemy adopting the exact position necessary for their impalement. As they might possibly have declined to be parties to their own destruction, in this case the rods were as likely to be a hindrance to the King's troops as damaging to the enemy. Our cavalier must have been considerably disgusted to find the kingdom delivered up without a struggle ; but, considering the then temper of the nation, it was perhaps the wisest course the King could have adopted.

In 1689 Mr. Blundell underwent, at Manchester, his fifth imprisonment, being confined with others of his religion, by virtue of a warrant from Lord Gerard of Brandon, Lord Lieutenant of the county. This step was no doubt taken as a measure of precaution to prevent the disaffected from joining King James in Ireland. This confinement lasted seven weeks, and was rendered less irksome by the company he met with. Of Mr. Towneley of Towneley, one of the prisoners, he says that his cheerful society would make life pleasant anywhere.

From the period of his release till the close of his life, Mr. Blundell remained at his own house, or rather within the tether of what he calls his five miles' chain.' This was the limit of travel then prescribed for recusants, who had to enter into recognisances not to exceed it without a licence. In January 1691, he thus writes to a Protestant friend in London :—

'Since my discharge at the assizes, I have not stirred from home ; yet my son and servant have made good use in my behalf (so far as their five miles' chain will reach) of those two horses for which you were kindly pleased to procure me a licence. We have now no disturbance at all, and if I be not greatly mistaken, all my friends here and hereabout are so sensible of this present ease, that they will not easily lose it through any demerit. It is but nine or ten months since my own in-foal mares were taken out of my grounds, and sold to my neighbours. Our colts were then taken at two or three years of age, and about that time it was, that my servant, return-ing unarmed from the next market, was assailed upon the road with pistol and bayonet, whereby some blood was drawn, because he would not yield his horse (which, in truth, was a very mean one) to an officer of our country's militia, who refused to show an order for seizing the same. We have none of these doings now. We may sit very securely under our own vines, and we have reason to pray for the King. I am sure without his favour (a favour, I confess, unexpected) we had all been a prey to the law, or, rather, perhaps, to the rabble.'

The record of the death of one of Mr. Blundell's tenants, in 1692, brings to light a re-markable proof of the patriotism and loyalty of our cavalier. This man, Robert Tomson, had been a seaman in the reign of Charles I., and had performed some conspicuous act of gallantry, for which Mr. Blundell gave him a free lease of his tenement in Little Crosby. The grant is thus re-corded in the tenants' book :—

24th June 1669. Gave unto Robert Tomson, the seaman, a lease gratis, for the great service he had done to his late Majesty in time of the war, which was truly great and remarkable in many respects.

H

We regret that we have not succeeded in finding any particulars of this deed.  The ingratitude
and injustice with which Mr. Blundell had been
treated enhance the generosity of this act.  Himself a great sufferer for his loyalty, he would not
allow an inferior man, who had done a service to
the King, to go without his reward, although his
own reduced fortunes could ill afford the sacrifice.

Another trial awaited Mr. Blundell, before his
long and eventful career came to a close.  He was
one of the Lancashire Catholics of position accused of participation in the sham plot of 1694.
The late Bishop Goss, in 'Manchester State Trials,'
which he edited for the Chetham Society from
papers at Crosby, gives the following account of
his transaction :—

> On Monday, July 30, 1694, at half-past five in the
> morning, three of the King's messengers, with two
> of the informers, invaded the hall at Crosby, with
> the intention of carrying off old Mr. Blundell.  As,
> however, he was then in his seventy-fifth year, and
> had been lame for many years, in consequence of
> the injuries he had received while fighting in the
> royal cause, they did not take him with them : but
> they carried off a case of pistols, two swords, and a
> fowling-piece, with seven horses and two hackney-
> saddles.  Mr. William Blundell, jun., having shown
> them to his father's room, left the house ; but, find-
> ing on his return that they carried off his horses, he
> went to Liverpool, to Mr. Norris of Speke, who

gave him into the custody of the Mayor, by whom he was handed over to Captain Baker, who sent him to Chester Castle and thence to London, where, having been examined, he was committed and taken to Newgate. None of the authorities concerned in this illegal arrest seem to have doubted the justice of committing the son for the supposed crime of the father.

The trial resulted in the acquittal of the prisoners, who were dismissed by the Judge with the injunction to 'go and sin no more:' a singularly inappropriate application of Scripture in the case of these much injured gentlemen.

The brave, loyal, and virtuous Cavalier whose life we have been attempting to sketch ended his days peaceably at Crosby Hall, on May 24, 1698, He was interred at Sefton Church, in the Blundell Chapel, where the bones of so many of his ancestors repose. He was succeeded in his estates by his son William Blundell, who only survived him a few years, dying in 1702. This gentleman's son Nicholas, who married the Honourable Frances, daughter of Marmaduke, third Lord Langdale, and died in 1737, was the last in the male line of this ancient race. The family succession was kept up through the marriage of Frances, surviving daughter and heiress of Nicholas, with Henry Peppard, Esq., of Drogheda, whose son Nicholas took, in 1772, the name of Blundell, and was an-

cestor to Colonel Nicholas Blundell, its present
worthy representative.  To the courtesy of this
gentleman our readers are indebted for whatever
pleasure or interest they may derive from the
perusal of these pages.

The following is the petition to King James II.
referred to above, which was prepared by the Cavalier, but never presented.  It is interesting as containing the summary of his claims upon the merciful
consideration of his sovereign.  It is headed—

### The Family of William Blundell.

The family of W. B. hath continued in yᵉ place
where it is now seated for very many generations,
during which time there is no memory left that any
son or daughter of yᵉ house hath professed any other
than yᵉ Roman Catholick Religion.  This hath been
yᵉ cause that since yᵉ pretended Reformation, it hath
suffered persecution for the same in an extraordinary
degree.  The story would be here over long : and
so much thereof as happened before our memory,
may be found by ancient writings, that give us an
account of many imprisonments of yᵉ ancestors of
yᵉ said W. B., viz. at Chester, Lancaster, and London ;
the begging of yᵉ real estate by sundry court favourites in Queen Elizabeth's dayes, and yᵉ seizure of
yᵉ moveable goods with yᵉ utter loss of yᵉ same in
later times.  The persecution occasioned by yᵉ late
plott, and especially the execution of yᵉ statute for
20*l.* per mensem, hath been an extraordinary damage
by reason it hath also involved and very sorely im-

poverisht y^e greatest part of his tenants. For whereas
W. B. is y^e Lord or owner of one small Lordship or
Manor consisting of forty houses or thereabouts,
there are not (thro y^e grace of God) any other but
Catholicks in it, except, peradventure, one or two
dayly labourers, w^ch being born in other places are
come to live there for work. And as it hath pleased
God to grant such grace to that neighbourhood
dureing a long persecution, His goodness has been
greatly remarkable to y^e kindred of W. B. which is
scattered farther abroad ; as appears by a list of one
hundred Catholic Priests and Religions of both sexes,
whereof seven of his own children and all y^e rest in
the 2nd, 3rd, and 4th degree ; many of which are
liveing and many dead. If none of these had renounced y^e world, it is probable that an extraordinary
great number of that kindred had engaged in defence of y^e Crown in our late unfortunate warrs.
And yet there has likewise been very many such,
and some of them greatly remarkable, whereas there
were none at all that fought on y^e Rebells' side.

It is known that W. B. himself was sorely maimed
in y^e service at y^e very beginning of y^e warr, in the
year 42, and that he was for y^e same divested of
goods and land ; which lands were sequestred and
wholly detained from him for y^e space of ten years,
and then were exposed to sale by virtue of a Rump
act. Yet true it is, that they were purchased in the
name of his friends with moneys which he himself
procured, for his own proper use and behoofe.

This case of sequestration and sale under a
monstrous pretence of delinquency, involved all y^e
visible fortunes of very many hundreds of other

Catholick familyes, as well as y$^e$ family abovesaid of W. B. ; altho it may be hard at y$^e$ present to find one other English subject liveing, that in other respects and according to his small quantum has suffered so much as he by loss of blood, imprisonment, decimation, and sundry other wayes.  There are liveing this present year, 1687–8, no fewer then 13 sons and daughters (besides the teeming wife of his most dutiful eldest son and som children already preferred) that are yet to be provided for out of his small estate : and this estate at y$^e$ present is so sorely charged, that altho y$^e$ family hath long subsisted in y$^e$ worst of times, it is now in danger to fail when y$^e$ times are good.

.  .  .  . It is very well known that y$^e$ small township abovesaid was many years remarked for these things,—

That it had not a beggar ;

That it had not an alehouse ;

That it had not a Protestant in it.

Yet our troubles have so much increased for some later years, that y$^e$ case as to y$^e$ matter of beggars is sorely changed.

This document reminds us that time brings about its revenges.  It is curious to find one who had suffered constant persecution and had experienced the severe displeasure of the Crown because he refused to become a Protestant, pleading the absence of Protestantism in himself, family, and township, as an argument likely to find favour with his sovereign.  It is perhaps still more curious to notice that after the lapse of two centuries things remain in this respect almost wholly unchanged. A direct descendant of the Cavalier, occupying his mansion and estate, can say at this day of his village, that there is neither beggar, alehouse, nor Protestant within it. This cannot altogether be spoken now of the *township*, although the truth is not far from it.

The village of Little Crosby lies on the northwest of the park, almost within shelter of its walls. Many of the cottages have been rebuilt of late years, and the place has a neat and clean appearance. The school is under charge of the Sisters of Charity of St. Vincent of Paul, with whose habit those who have travelled abroad will be familiar. One of the sisters of the present squire is a member of this religious Order. The church stands at the northern extremity of the village, and is the result of a bequest of the late William Blundell, Esq., who died in 1854. This gentleman married Katharine, daughter of Sir Thomas Massey Stanley, Bart., of Hooton, Cheshire, the chief of that famous race.

Little Crosby Church is a neat Gothic edifice, complete with spire, &c. The interior decorations were designed and executed by the patient and skilful hand of the present squire in his younger years.

## CHAPTER IV.

### CHARACTER AND LITERARY PRODUCTIONS OF WILLIAM BLUNDELL.

*Character seen in his Writings—Confidence reposed in him
—His Good-humour—As a Soldier—His Influence over
Young Men—Tutor to his Grandsons—Religious Mat-
ters—Difficulties in the Way of practising Religion—
Rev. John Walton, S.J.—Rev. Francis Waldegrave, S.J.
—Relations with his Chaplains—Their Position in the
Household—Agreeable Companions—Promoters of Mar-
riages—A Curious Love-letter—Priests of Good Birth—
Large Number of his Relatives Religious—Real Names
not entered in Pedigrees—His Literary Occupations—
Common-place Books—Plan of Drexelius—Favourite
Authors—Neglect of Poetry—Unacquainted with Shake-
speare's or Milton's Verses—Character of his Remarks—
Wise Suggestions—Letters intended for Publication—
Treatise on Penal Laws.*

THE following notes show that Mr. Blundell possessed much of that honourable and open character
which is said to belong to Lancashiremen of the
best type. He speaks his mind in a straightfor-
ward, manly way. The impression we have in
reading his letters and remarks is highly favourable
to his integrity. We seem to be listening to a

man who would rather suffer any torments than tell a lie or deny his principles. And that such was his real character, the whole tenor of his life bears witness. His friends reposed the greatest confidence in him, and he was frequently selected as umpire in family differences, where the circumstances called for the exercise of much tact and judgment. Ladies who presided over religious houses abroad found in him a faithful financial agent. His carefulness and exactitude in managing this troublesome business, which he undertook solely out of charity, is manifest from the account-books which he has left behind him. Considering the many troubles in which he was involved, it is difficult to see how he contrived to bring up a large family in tolerable comfort. He says in one of his letters, that three generations of his race were then living on the estate, and that he does not believe that there is in Lancashire another housekeeper who has so many mouths to feed. One element in his character was of the most essential service to him at all times, and that was his unfailing good-humour. Whatever he had to endure, he never desponded ; nor did he give way to any murmuring or repining at Divine Providence. How he combated temptations of this nature (which happened to him as to others), may be gathered from some of the following reflections.

I

He was of a hasty temperament, and frequently yielded to sallies of anger. This propensity, however, he much subdued by watchfulness, and we learn from his own observations, how continually he laboured to repress other excesses, not by general resolutions, but by particular and approved methods. His witty and agrèeable manner made him a delightful companion, and his society was eagerly sought for by a large circle of acquaintance. He reckoned amongst his dearest friends many who were not of his own faith, and exercised towards all an hospitality that was only bounded by his means.

If his career as a soldier had not been cut short, Mr. Blundell was likely to have proved a good commander. He was of an enterprising, hardy, and valorous nature : qualities which would have gone far to endear him to his troops. Nor was he wanting in that discretion and ability without which a general can neither combat difficulties nor achieve successes. To the close of his life he took much interest in military matters, and made many observations relative to cannon and other implements of war. As has been already remarked, one of his latest letters, addressed to the Vice-Chamberlain of King James II.'s consort, contained details of a plan for the defeat of the Prince of Orange's troop of horse.

His letters are no hasty scrawls, but bear marks of the careful revision of the writer. They must have been charming reading to his correspondents, from the pleasant vein of humour which runs through them. One addressed to a recently married daughter, which he wrote towards the end of his life, is full of fun, showing that he retained to the last the same happy and contented mind. They contain many proofs of the influence which he possessed over young men of his own position in life, and of the excellent use which he made of that influence. Whilst his neighbours, the young squires of Ince Blundell and Scarisbrick, are still at college, he writes to them in his pleasant manner, giving them details of country news, but does not fail to exhort them to lay up such a stock of learning and virtue as will enable them to combat the temptations to which they will soon find themselves exposed. His nephew, Thomas Selby of Biddlestone, Northumberland, Esq., who had come early into possession of his estate, experienced a large share of this tenderness and solicitude. In a long letter written to him at St. Omer's College, he confesses his own mistakes in early life, the better to warn him against those dangers which beset unguarded youth. He uses many motives to urge his correspondent to aim at a high standard, while he enjoys the advantage of residing at a place so renowned for virtue and learning. One sentence we give as a sample of his earnest and impressive manner :

> I would have you, nephew, to think often (it is a lawful and honourable ambition), that the time will come when you shall sit like an oracle in the High-lands of Northumberland, giving counsel and assist-ance to all your friends and neighbours. So did Roger Widdrington, your late neighbour and kins-man, who, besides a general reputation for wisdom, raised himself merely by his own wit, tempered finely with learning and seconded by a commend-able frugality, from a most inconsiderable to a fair and eminent fortune. This example is familiar (*nam nota loquor*), and yourself cannot choose but remember him.

It may be thought that this was the outcome of the wisdom of his riper age, but he had only attained his thirtieth year when he penned these lines. They represent, therefore, the excellent form which his mind had thus early assumed. So great an interest did he take in the welfare of youth, that for some years he acted as tutor to his grand-sons Edmond and Richard Butler, the children of Lord Mountgarret. His assiduity and perse-verance in this laborious office were incessant. The result he communicates in a letter to their father, in which he commends the proficiency of his pupils, and boasts, not unreasonably, that this success has been attained without the help of a rod. He says that he had found better means of stimulating their industry, and urges their father to send them abroad, to pursue their studies under a better master. He says of the elder—

> I would have him to dance and fence, to speak Latin and French readily, and to see the world. We are here so far from speaking good Latin, that our English is barbarous. You may find us now and then up to our ears in Plutarch, in a hot dispute whether Alexander the Great or Cæsar was the braver man. And perhaps, within an hour or two afterwards, the gallant fierce disputant will be up to the knees in the brambles, at the head of a whole regiment of our pitiful tatterdemalions, beating to start a hare. I blame not but pity him for it ; he hath seldom better company with which to divert himself. And yet, to my great admiration, he contracts as little rusticity as any I have ever met with in so hard a case.

The elder of these youths became, in 1706, the sixth Viscount Mountgarret, and retained to the close of his life a strong attachment to Crosby, the scene of his happy and careless boyhood. When obliged to leave Ireland, through the troubles in which his family was involved by its fidelity to King James, he sought with his father an asylum in England. They settled in the neighbouring town of Ormskirk, then the residence of a number of the local gentry, as the petty capital of a rural

district.   Edmund, Lord Mountgarret, was restored
in blood and honours in 1721.

In matters of religion, as may easily be discovered from the following notes, Mr. Blundell was
not only staunch in belief, but faithful in the practice of the duties of his creed.   And yet he must
have had many difficulties to encounter in securing
opportunities for its observances.   At a time when
no Catholic chapel except the Queen's, and those
of foreign ambassadors, were tolerated in England,
the services of the Church were necessarily performed in secret in some obscure part of the
dwelling.   To this the tenants and neighbouring
Catholics had access, and the priest attended to
their spiritual wants with as much precaution as
possible.   All this was accompanied with great
risk to the host, and still greater to the priest, whose
life was at the mercy of the meanest informant.
The chaplain had generally, for greater security,
his room at the upper part of the house, and in
time of danger was obliged to keep very close and
retired.   Mr. Blundell, in his letters to Haggerston,
often desires to be remembered to the gentleman
at the 'top of the house.'   Here too he was, when
necessary, served from the family table.   In the
' Breiffe Narration ' of Rev. Gilbert Blackhall (published in 1844 by the Spalding Club), the writer
says—' In great houses, if the priests eat in their

private chambers, they must stay till the lady send them from the table, upon trenchers, such pieces as she pleaseth. I have seen this done in England to priests eating in their chambers' (1638). A frequent change of residence was very necessary, and we do not find that any priests had a settled abode till the close of the civil war. Curiously enough, it happens that Crosby Hall is the first place in Lancashire named in conjunction with a resident priest. The Rev. John Walton, S.J., became Mr. Blundell's chaplain about 1652, but was obliged to leave through ill-health in 1656. Mr. Blundell, who was then staying with his wife at Haggerston, sent him a farewell letter, which we quote, to show the affectionate relations subsisting between them :

I received your letter of farewell long since, and if y$^u$ had dealt lesse cruelly by writing lesse kindly, I could sooner have returned an answer. That part w$^{ch}$ belongs to my wife, she returns y$^u$ in prayers and tears ; but those (as y$^u$ know best) are generally much wanting in her husband. Yet I confidently believe now that he prayes very heartily amongst other blessings for your health. Just so do I pray for my purgatory in this world, both wishing and fearing y$^e$ smart. If y$^u$ recover now, S$^r$, we would not murther y$^u$ againe at Crosby for all y$^e$ world. If y$^u$ linger in y$^e$ same maner still, I have petitioned y$^{ur}$ master to return y$^u$ thither. And as long as those fearefull hopes of ours are lyk to continew, so long shall y^{ur} poore old cabin be undisposed to any other, &c.

The Rev. John Walton, S.J., who belonged to an old Lancashire family, was sent on the mission in 1652, and it is probable that Crosby was the first place that he served. When absent from home, for the reasons already assigned, we find Mr. Blundell saying in a letter to his sister Frances at Crosby, in 1656, ' Mr. Walton is welcome to stay and do nothing ; ' from which it would appear that his health was very bad. He did not return to Crosby ; but died in London on December 30, 1677, at the age of fifty-five. The next chaplain at Crosby was the Rev. Francis Waldegrave, S.J. He was a great grandson of Sir Edward Waldegrave, Knight, the stout servant of Queen Mary, who was imprisoned for refusing to enforce the mandate of King Edward VI.'s Council, which forbade the celebration of mass at Copped Hall, in Essex, the then residence of the Princess. Losing his father in early youth, his mother, Lucy, daughter of Dean Mervin, sought an asylum with her brother, a clergyman of the Established Church. Notwithstanding her conversion, he received her and her children with the utmost kindness, and made no objection to her son Francis going to St. Omer's College, which was accomplished with the assistance of his aunt Frances, who had married Richard,

Lord Weston, Lord High Treasurer of England, and subsequently, Earl of Portland. He was ordained priest in the church of St. John Lateran, at Rome, on March 25, 1651, and left college for the English Mission in the autumn of the following year. After three years he embraced the Society of Jesus, having long had this desire. Mr. Blundell says that he was the dear friend of his brother Richard, who had the same desire, and, impatient of delay, sought the intercession of several cardinals to obtain a dispensation from his College oath. Making many journeys for the object through the streets of Rome, during the summer heats of 1649, he contracted a fever, of which he died the same year. He had the consolation of being clothed, before his death, with the habit of St. Ignatius. In another place will be found Mr. Blundell's memoir of his brother, from which it appears that he was a youth of remarkable virtue and ability. After having served Crosby for many years, Father Waldegrave went to Lydiate Hall, the residence of old Mrs. Ireland, where he died in 1701. He was buried in the ruined chapel of St. Katharine, and a copy of the inscription, still to be seen on his tombstone, will be found in ' Foley's Records, S.J.,' vol. v. He was a man of zeal and talent, and Mr. Blundell contracted a friendship with him which lasted through life. After he had left Crosby, his friend continued to employ him as his spiritual director, and consulted him in weighty matters.   He speaks of a horse to which he had given the name of ' Waldegrave.'

The amusing incident which Mr. Blundell relates of his chaplain refusing, on one occasion, to join him and his family in a particular act of devotion, no doubt refers to Mr. Waldegrave.   It did not, however, disturb the amicable relations subsisting between them, and the squire's momentary irritation passed off in the act of recording it. There is no doubt that, although priests had only their patrons to look to for the supply of all their wants, yet they occupied a perfectly independent position in the household.   They were by no means that abject servile class which chaplains of the Established Church are represented by some popular writers to have been.   They were, for the most part, men of family, often the equals in point of birth to those at whose table they sat, and not rarely their superiors in culture and learning.   Add to this the advantages derived from a long residence abroad, and it may readily be imagined that a Catholic squire of those days found in his chaplain a polished and agreeable companion.   Moreover, their wide acquaintance with the Catholic gentry would furnish them with topics of conversation very acceptable to those knit together by the powerful bonds of faith and mutual suffering. Much information on family matters was thus obtained, and introductions with a view to marriage were frequently furnished through their agency. When Mr. Blundell wanted a wife for his son and heir, he received very exact particulars of two matches proposed to him, and in one case his informant was a priest. Although his choice did not fall upon either of these parties, yet he was indebted to a priest for an introduction to his future daughter-in-law. In a letter to the Rev. Henry Heaton, S.J. (probably Lord Montague's chaplain), he takes occasion to thank him for the good wife which he had procured for his son. This lady was Mary, daughter of Rowland Eyre, of Hassop, Derbyshire, Esq., who married William Blundell in 1668. We are tempted to bring to light a love-letter, written shortly before their union, which tends to show the immense distance between that age and the present one. The courtly and chivalrous terms in which this Cavalier's son greets the lady of his heart will fall on modern ears like the strains of an ancient roundelay.

It is near ten days since I was torn away from your presence, where I desire ever to live, having left my heart behind me. Yet I bear the separation with the less impatience, because you did not reject me when I came from thence. I shall never desire to

live without your favour, nor shall your favours ever
raise me to a higher degree of confidence than becomes your humble servant. This paper shall take
the boldness to kiss your fair hand, from whence I
am encouraged to hope for such a favourable return
as may keep my hopes alive. I will still confide in
your goodness to allow me the great honour to
appear again in your presence about the middle of
the next month. Oh ! my most honoured dear
lady, how shall I count those unkind hours that
keep me from so great a joy ! I could wish your
heart like mine in all but the pain it feels. I told
you once before (as I hope I did not offend), that
your goodness hath cause to. pardon what your
virtue and beauty have done.

The accomplished object of these stately sighs
brought her husband a numerous family, but was
always delicate in health, and was more than once
on the brink of the grave. In her youth she had
wished to consecrate herself to God in religion, but
yielded to the representation of her friends, who
thought her health too infirm for such a vocation.
On the death of her husband in 1702, her longing
for a religious life returned, and she went to join
the Benedictine Nuns at Ghent, where two of her
daughters had been professed. One of these was the
Superioress, and under her rule she spent happily
the last years of her pilgrimage. She died in 1707,
and a sitting portrait of her in her religious habit
is amongst the family pictures at Crosby Hall.

We have said that the priests in the times we are alluding to were frequently men of good birth, and Mr. Blundell names no fewer than eighty-seven of his relatives, without reckoning any of his own family, who had embraced a religious life. In speaking of the disastrous civil wars and the large number of Catholics who had fallen on the royal side, he says that the number would have been much greater if so many had not entered a better militia. Out of a family of three sons and seven daughters who grew to man's estate, two sons and five daughters of our Cavalier became religious. Taking together the three generations in the midst of which he stood, no less than seventeen Blundells, male and female, devoted themselves to a religious life. Unless the sons of the gentry had adopted this vocation, the necessary succession of priests, humanly speaking, could not have been kept up. By debarring Catholic gentlemen from any worldly employment suitable to their position in life, the Government, in its blind policy, promoted to the best of its power the cause of that religion which it was its object to stifle. It threw into its arms those who alone had the means and the opportunity of becoming priests. Moreover, it furnished a class of priests which in the circumstances of the times was more acceptable to the gentry, and therefore more serviceable to religion, than any other could have been. Not the least valuable portion of the work to which we have already alluded (' Foley's Records, S.J.'), is the revelation it makes of the real names of the priests whose lives it recounts. It will there be seen that they worked under assumed names, not only on account of the danger which threatened themselves, but also for fear of that in which their kindred might be involved through their means. For this reason priests and religious were carefully excluded from pedigrees presented at Visitations or entrusted to Heralds' College. Many ancient and honourable houses will be able to fill up these lacunæ in their genealogical tables by the aid of the pedigrees in which Brother Foley introduces, for the first time, not the least worthy branches of their stock.

We must now devote a short space to some cursory notice of the literary occupations of Mr. Blundell. These pervaded his life, or rather a certain calm and studious life ran alongside his public troubled career, tending much, no doubt, to sweeten the cup of his sorrows. He seems to have begun the practice of taking notes from the various authors he read when about the age of forty. These notes are contained in three books, called ' Historia,' ' Adversaria,' and ' Hodge Podge.' The two first are small quartos of perhaps 1200 pages each, and these are for the most part well filled, and closely written in a neat and clear hand. 'Hodge Podge' is a large quarto, and, in addition to Mr. Blundell's notes, contains literary productions in poetry and prose of his grandfather, besides matters of later date. Most of the extracts and notes have a Latin heading in the margin, and the same heading recurs in several places, if the number of selections requires it. This plan of commonplace book has obvious advantages. With a general threefold grouping there is ample scope to embrace every subject within very elastic folds. Although he nowhere mentions it, it seems highly probable that Mr. Blundell adopted this plan from 'Drexelius' a learned Jesuit writer of the early part of the seventeenth century. It is certain that he was well acquainted with his treatise called 'Aurofodina,' in which this system is recommended and elucidated by examples. He quotes at the beginning of ' Historia ' the Latin dictum found in this work, and followed it in practice, ' Modo tui armenti pecus sit, de stabulo non litigemus : ' ' Only let it be one of your herd, and you need not care where it is housed.' This plan of common-place book has found favour with many literary men. William Windham, the statesman, had his ' Historia ' and ' Adversaria,' as we learn from his diary (a very disappointing book), and it is highly probable that Dr. Johnson, to whom he deferred in such matters, recommended to him the adoption of this system. The result in Mr. Blundell's case is an accumulation of extracts and quotations, which, while they bespeak his industry, must have helped materially to enlarge his knowledge and correct his judgment. Common-place books are of all publications the most dreary and uninviting, and hence it happens that even the names of Southey and Buckle cannot invest their compilations of this kind with any flavour of interest. We need not stop, therefore, to speak of these selections, which derive whatever value they possess from the books from which they were taken. These are now for the most part obsolete, yet it is a pleasure to find that Mr. Blundell appreciated the writings of Bacon, the great luminary of his age. He quotes Ben Jonson, Sidney, and numberless travellers in whose strange accounts of newly discovered regions he much delighted. Such descriptions have no longer any interest, but the raciness and originality of 'Howell's Letters of Foreign Travel,' a work frequently quoted by Mr. Blundell, have preserved it from oblivion. In one of his amusing 'Roundabout Papers,' Thackeray says, 'Montaigne and Howell's Letters are my bedside books. If I wake at night, I have one or other of them to prattle me to sleep again.' In religious books he had some special favourites ; such as the

'Holy Court,' by Caussin, a work that has still many readers, who gather instruction from its ample pages, and regale themselves with its numerous examples. He was well versed in the Holy Scriptures, and applies them frequently in illustration of various headings. Although Mr. Blundell was in his younger days the author of verses by no means despicable, yet he seems early to have abandoned the pursuit. It is quite in conformity with his character to suppose that he relinquished poetry from a religious motive, for fear of it engrossing too much of his mind and time. With the same view, probably, he gave up all desire of seeing plays or comedies, or even of reading such productions. At all events, he very rarely quotes any of them, and considering the general character of such writings in the seventeenth century, no one can say that he did not practise a wise abstinence. Yet it probably deprived him of the opportunity of reading Shakespeare's inimitable works, with which he appears to have been wholly unacquainted. He only mentions his name once, and that in connection with the worst of his plays. Shakespeare's fame was of slow growth, and he cannot be said to have been really known to his countrymen till the opening years of last century. Even the Rev. John Ward, who became Vicar of Stratford-on-Avon in 1662, has very little to say

L

in his diary of the man to whom that town is indebted for whatever celebrity it possesses. One passage seems to corroborate the opinion that Shakespeare had little classical learning, but he was evidently then unacquainted with his plays, for he adds this memorandum, 'Remember to peruse Shakespeare's plays, and be much versed in them, that I may not be ignorant in that matter.' Still it is remarkable that a gentleman in the position of Mr. Blundell, a literary man, not unacquainted with the contents of London bookshelves, and accustomed to polished if not learned society, should know nothing whatever of our great household poet. With his contemporary Milton, as a poet, he was no better acquainted. Of his prose works he speaks frequently, and, as may be imagined, with due abhorrence ; but he does not seem to have had any idea that he was the most charming versifier in the kingdom.

The foregoing remarks do not apply to the following notes added by Mr. Blundell himself, which form the matter now given to the public. These are the product of his own thought and observation, and are generally very judicious. He expresses himself in clear and concise terms, free from affectation or pedantry. His good sense revolted against the fashion, common to writers of his day, of decking out their sentences in gaudy trappings. He says of one book ('Loveday's Letters'), that if it was put into plain English, it would look like a plucked peacock. The anecdotes which he recounts are well told, and the quaintness of their dress reminds us of his contemporary Pepys. Several of them regard historical personages, and their authenticity is ensured by Mr. Blundell's careful habit of giving dates and names. His position in life afforded him opportunities of seeing and hearing much that has more than a local interest. Thus he speaks of the conversations of Charlotte, Countess of Derby, the famous defender of Latham House. Unfortunately, he does not tell us many of her remarks, which may have arisen from the difficulty which he says he had in catching her observations 'by defect of my Lady's English.'

It will be seen that in many matters of political economy Mr. Blundell was much in advance of his age. He advocates the publication of law reports and of the proceedings in criminal cases, and has an eye to the advantage, if not necessity, of advertising. Notices of sales, &c., he recommends should be put up at the church door or village smithy. He thinks it advisable that when a gentleman wants to sell his horse, a ribbon should be affixed to the bridle. In days when everybody rode on horseback, it is strange that so good a suggestion was never adopted. He speaks of the advantage of circulating the particulars of the accidents that may happen in a neighbourhood, and instances the case of a man who, while digging for rabbits at the Grange, was smothered by the sand falling upon him. Shortly after, a similar disaster occurred at Maghull, which is only three miles distant. ' Surely,' he says, ' this would never have happened if the last man had been aware of the other's mishap.' He had the satisfaction of finding one at least of his recommendations carried out before his death. His position in life and well-known integrity had caused him to be the depositary of various sums of money, belonging to the ladies who presided over religious houses abroad. This money he was in the habit of lending to gentlemen of his acquaintance in sums of 50*l.* at the invariable interest of six per cent. He sometimes found a difficulty in locating these trusts, and thought the establishment of agencies for the lending and borrowing of money would be of much benefit. Such houses were afterwards established in a few provincial towns, and he made use of them in his later years. The parties who undertook the management of this business appear to have been at first agents or attorneys. The system of banking was commenced in London before the end of the seventeenth century, and Mr. Blundell frequently quotes the works of Sir Josiah Child on trade and currency questions. The cavalier's suggestion of a matrimonial mart, conducted by ' sober and discreet persons,' is a good one, and such institutions are successful in France. In this country they have not been attempted, perhaps through fear of the ridicule which might be thrown upon them. It is well known that the more vulgar method of advertising has given rise frequently to practical jokes not of the most gentle character. In the matter of weights and measures Mr. Blundell had the sagacity to see that great injustice and anomalies might be remedied by a law of uniformity. It is very remarkable that abuses which this country gentleman saw and spoke of 200 years ago have been permitted to go on to the present day. This very year has witnessed for the first time the attempt to supply the obvious remedy for a great evil which he so long ago suggested.

In addition to the notes of Mr. Blundell which are here given, he left behind him a number of his own letters copied into folio sheets, and since bound up in a volume. He has also inserted in another book those letters of his correspondents which he deemed worthy of preservation. His letters are uniformly well written, and there are few of them that will not bear perusal. In these days of railway haste, correspondence has become an extinct art, and one not likely to be revived. If the present publication meet with the favour of the public, it is intended to publish these letters as the second series of the 'Crosby Records,' under the title of 'A Cavalier's Letter Book.' We have already in the present introduction given a few extracts from some of these letters for the purpose of illustrating the life of our hero.

A formal work of Mr. Blundell's, entitled 'A Short Treatise on the Penal Laws,' exists in MS. at Crosby, but a printed copy cannot be found, though he states that a few copies were printed in London. It is a small quarto containing about eighty-five pages, and giving an account of the laws affecting religion and of the hardships arising from them. The author argues that the Catholics are entitled to relief by reason of their great loyalty. He proves this from the fact that, whereas the Catholic gentry of the kingdom were computed before the wars at one-fifteenth of the whole, no less than one-third or one-fourth of the officers of the King's army were Catholics. The majority of those in command who fell at Worcester, he believes to have been Catholics. A good deal of space is taken up in replying to the extravagances of Prynne and others.

In 1876–7 the Manx Society published 'A

History of the Isle of Man, by Wm. Blundell, Esq., of Crosby, co. Lancaster, 1648–56,' in two volumes, edited by Wm. Harrison, Esq., and forming Nos. 25 and 27 of the series. The original MS. from which the transcript possessed by the Society was made, appears to be in the Knowsley library. The materials used in the compilation of this work were collected by Mr. Blundell in 1648, when he visited the island under the following circumstances, as recorded in his preface :—' Wearied with being so often wakened at midnight to fly from the King's and Parliamentary troops, both equally feared because equally plundering, and finding no shelter under the Snowden Hills, I resolved to banish myself to the Isle of Man.' The Editor mentions in his introduction that Seacome (John Seacome was house-steward to William, ninth Earl of Derby) alludes to this work in his ' Account of the Isle of Man,' appended to his ' History of the House of Stanley,' and styles the author ' the great and learned Mr. Blundell of Crosby.' He characterises it as the clearest and most correct account of the History and Antiquities of the Island. There does not appear to be a copy of the above MS. at Crosby, and it is somewhat singular that neither in the following notes, nor in the whole series of his letters (occupying three hundred folio pages), does Mr. Blundell make any mention of this history, which he must have completed early in life during the days of his sequestration.

The spelling in Mr. Blundell's MS. notes is generally good, but we have for the most part accommodated it to modern rules. In other respects nothing has been altered, and with the exception of the omission sometimes of a redundant parenthesis, the construction of the sentences remains precisely as he left it.

The editor wishes to express his acknowledgments to J. E. Bailey, Esq., F.S.A., of Stretford, Manchester, for the notes with which he has favoured him, and which are marked with his initials.

T. E. GIBSON.

6 CROSBY ROAD,
BIRKDALE, SOUTHPORT.

A

# CAVALIER'S NOTE-BOOK.

A

# CAVALIER'S NOTE-BOOK.

———◆◇◆———

NOTE such things as are more like to be service- Electio scri-bendorum. able many years after the noting than about the present time.  For young men do collect such things as to their riper years do appear but toys ; therefore be sure to make your notes a little more weighty (i.e. of matters somewhat higher) than your present genius and inclination can yet fully relish.  Time will bring you to the liking and the use of those which otherwise would be tedious and fruitless.

Collect only the best things, even a few of the very best, to avoid contempt of your own collections no less than confusion.

Do not forbear to note because you know not unto what letter or class to reduce the thing most properly ; be sure to insert it.  '*Modo tui armenti pecus sit, de stabulo non litigemus'* (Only let it be one of your herd, and you need not care where it is housed).

I did not begin to take these notes until July 15, 1659, being that day 39 years old, yet some few in the 'Historia' were notes which I first took in loose papers about the year 1644 and 1645. *Quantum tempus perdidimus!*

Admonitio fidelis amici.

Few there are who will give or take advice as they ought. I have oft been grievously discouraged in the freedom of my admonishments given to grave persons, men of great virtue and learning, and even sometimes when I had not given the admonishment till themselves had desired me to do it. If such men as these did take my plain dealing so ill, what may be thought of such as myself? Perhaps I have offended so oft in taking admonitions unthankfully, that now, by reason of my pride, I meet with few or none.

This will remind the reader of a well-known passage in Dr. Johnson's 'Life' in connection with his friend Langton.

Turres altiores.

On June 3, 1676, I ascended the new tower or monument at Pudding Lane, London, by 310 steps (which I twice counted), to the noble iron balcony which is round the tower ; from whence I had an excellent view of the town and country. Above this balcony, the tower, not then quite finished, is raised (as I once counted them), 136 steps. This I take to be the intended full height of the tower. I take the steps on the lower parts to be 6½ inches, but 6 inches from about the middle. They are large and fine, wonderfully held up by ironwork, after the mode of the stairs at Greenwich. The base of the tower is near 26½ feet square. But the tower is round and *egregie structa*, all of stone.

June 3, 1676. I saw about 120 brass guns on the Tower Hill, London. One weighed, as by the figures, 8.1.27. The length appeared to be near 13 feet ; the wideness, by my span, 7½ inches. It was said to carry a ball of 63 pounds. *Tormenta cærulea.*

The way to establish trade is to establish fair dealing. Of merchandise some sorts consist of 100 to the hundred, others of 120 and 112. Note the words of 'The Complete Tradesman,' printed 1680 for John Dunton, viz., '70 pipe-hoops, 90 hogshead, 120 barrel or kilderkin, 110 pink or *Mercatores.*

firkin-hoops make a hundred;' glass bottles 21 to
the dozen, &c.  One agreed to deliver 100 measures
of salt for so many hundreds of oats.  He took the
numbers to be equal, but it was adjudged otherwise
at Liverpool, as I have heard, to his great damage.
A stone of beef is 8 lbs., of horseman's weight 14,
of wool 16, 20, and in some parts of Northumberland 23½.

Eleemo-
synæ.

It was the opinion of Judge Hale (see p. 3 in
his ' Life '), that to give to such poor as did receive
alms of the parish, was to save so much money to
the rich, who were bound by law to keep them.
He therefore gave to the poor housekeepers who
were not kept on the charge of the parish.  He
laid aside the tenth penny of all he got for the
poor.  *Ibid.* p. 89.

The present January 5, 1686–7, I saw a lusty,
strong beggar woman in the street at Wildhouse
Gate, who carried upon her back, in a begging way,
an old woman, which she said was her mother, and
that she was 102 years old.  She said that she
lived in St. Ann's Parish of Soho.  I told her the
parish was hard-hearted to permit such way of
begging, and she did say thereupon that the parish

was the most hard-hearted in the world. She got money and farthings apace while I stood by her, and my man Walter Thelwall (who writes this after my dictate) did afterwards meet her in the same street, and saw her receive in a very short time alms from six or seven persons, most of which gave her halfpence, and the rest each one farthing.

Sir Roger Bradshaigh limed the hall croft with lime from Clitheroe, which cost about 8*l.* per acre, each horse-load being 1*s.* 10*d.* It hath yielded very good corn since that time, which is now about twelve years, and is like to continue. One year barley, one year fallows, one year wheat for the most part. 1660.

*(margin note:* Liming of land.*)*

Out of Mr. Foxe's note, who got limestones for me in Wales, 1659—

|  | *s.* | *d.* |
|---|---|---|
| For getting 12 load of stone at 2*d.* per load | 2 | 0 |
| ,, carriage of do. | 17 | 0 |
| ,, slack to burn it 4*s.*, and for carriage 4*s.* | 8 | 0 |
| ,, burning all at 4*d.* per load  .  . | 4 | 0 |

Sir Roger Bradshaigh, of Haigh, near Wigan, born 1627, created Bart. 1679, was the son and heir of James Bradshaigh, Esq., a remarkably learned and pious man, who died in his father's lifetime. His mother was Anne, daughter of Sir William Norris,

of Speke, but he had the misfortune to lose his
parents, who were both Catholics, in very early life.
His guardian, John Fleetwood, of Penwortham,
Esq., entrusted his education to the Earl of Derby,
by whom he was brought up a Protestant.   He was
throughout life devotedly attached to his cousin
Mr. Blundell, and performed for him all the kind
offices (and they were very many) which a friendly
Protestant could do for one lying constantly under
the pressure of the penal laws.   Sir Roger died
March 31, 1684, and the baronetcy expired in 1731,
on the death of Sir Roger Bradshaigh, fourth Bart.
The property fell through female heiresses to the
family of the present Earl of Crawford and Balcarres,
one of whose residences is Haigh Hall, the fine
mansion of the Bradshaighs, in the neighbourhood
of Wigan.   This nobleman also possesses the extensive and valuable coalfields with which the estate
abounds.

Masons'
work.

A mason will commonly demand for the getting, working, and setting of such window-work as
that in my new building, about 6*d.* the foot.   How
great their gain will be, we may judge by this.
Daniel Sefton (as his prentice told me), doth work
upon one day 12 feet of stanchions for those windows, and that in November.   It is true that it is
the easiest sort of work in my windows, but the
said prentice at the same time of the year did
work, as he told me, 5 feet of jambs upon one day.

And his master doubtless is able to work more than he can. A.D. 1660. But note, the said Daniel, when I hired him by days' wages, did usually work no more (and commonly not so much) than 6 feet of stanchions of the very same stone and the same mould.

I have heard that the wallers about Rivin Pike will make a defensible rough wall for 9*d.* or 10*d.* the rood. Inquire of this, for Daniel demandeth more than twice as much.

Hair, if it is grey, may be made black, or of a good dark colour, by rubbing with the light dust of cork which is burnt to ashes. The hair will continue that colour three or four days at the least. You may work the same effect in this manner upon red hair. It likewise drieth the hair exceedingly, and is done in an instant. You must slice the cork very thin, and it will take fire and flame and burn quickly into the powder abovesaid. I saw it tried by Mr. Stanton, November 8, 1660. *Hair, to colour ;*

The tops of green hemp ready to knot or seed, being made into a juice and mixed with cream and olive oil, is singular good to anoint the parts from where your hair is apt to fall, to prevent falling. *to grow.*

N

*Idem narravit*, who hath tried the same, and doth think it causeth hair to come thicker.

Burn southernwood to ashes and mix therewith either thick salad oil, or, which is better, the oil of black snails: anoint the bald part evening and morning, often. This or nothing will make hair to grow upon a bald place. Mr. Stanton had this from Dr. Martin, who magnified the secret very much. The southernwood must be well dried by the fire or the sun. Let it then take fire and burn in an earthen pot of itself almost a day together, still stirring up (if it need), to burn the better. The snails must have salt sprinkled among them, and being then hung up in a net, they will work themselves into a fat, which will drop into a dish which you may set under it.

Statura hominis.

I was present in the ship (about five miles from Dover), two or three hours before King Charles II. landed in England on Fryday, May 25, 1660, when the King (by reason of an accident), took his own measure, standing under a beam in the cabin, upon which place he made a mark with a knife. Sundry tall persons went under it, but there were none that could reach it. After all I went under it myself, and turning in the ends of my thumb and my little finger, I set the knuckle of my thumb, stretched out as much as could be, upon my head, and turning the knuckle of my little finger (borne up as stiff as might be), I found it did touch directly the mark which the King had made. So that I find myself to be about 5 inches lower than that mark, and I think I am 3 inches lower, as I stand in my high-heeled shoe, than I was before I was lame.

In November 1861, I saw an Irish stripling called (as I take it) Edmund Malone, said to be then under 17 years of age. I found him to be higher than John Dodes by about 1½ inch. I think he was 7 ft. 2½ in. in his shoes, which were not high. He was languid and listless, and not comely, although he was straight. I was told he died a few days or weeks after.

On May 23, 1660, the King embarked at the Hague on board a vessel which had hitherto been called the 'Naseby,' but to which he now gave the name of the 'Royal Charles,' and landed at noon on 25th, at Dover, where Monk awaited him surrounded by an immense crowd.—(' Lady of Latham,' by Madme. Guizot de Witt, p. 244.)

On August 20, 1675, Mr. Blundell of Ince Juramenta.

N 2

told me that the King (within four months of that time) had said that Lancashire was infamous for perjury and packing of juries. These words, or words to this effect, my cousin Blundell said to me as we came from Croxteth.

> This was Henry son of Robert Blundell, of Ince Blundell, Esq., who had succeeded to the estate on the death of his father in 1656. He spoke feelingly on the subject of juries, having himself lost in 1665 a large tract of land, and been mulcted in costs and mesne profits, as the issue of a law-suit with the Gerards, Earls of Macclesfield, on a dispute concerning the boundaries of adjoining properties purchased by the two families. Some account of this tedious and expensive contest will be found in 'Lydiate Hall and its Associations.' Mr. Blundell seems to have thought that the power and might of his opponent influenced the adverse verdict of the jury. He married Bridget daughter of the famous Cavalier Sir Thomas Tildesley, Knt., and died on March 30, 1687–8, at the age of 55.

Oratio.

While I am in health, I may do well to make and write down a prayer, protestation, or soliloquy, just such a one as I would desire to say in the extremity of my last sickness. By this I may renounce all thoughts, words, and deeds contrary to a good Christian, which shall happen or to which I shall be tempted at the time. I may beg of

God to assist my soul while my body lies in torment, and, by the extreme anguish thereof, hath stupefied or perverted my reason. I may beg likewise grace for my friends that stand by to assist me, that they may not be scandalised either at the rage or stupidity which then may happen unto me by the force of the sickness. And I may offer myself up to suffer more and longer torments, if it be God's pleasure I should do so ; and that grace may be allowed me to bear them, I may carry this paper always about me, to the end it may be read to me in my sickness.

The recent admirable biography of Thomas Grant, first Bishop of Southwark, by the lady who writes under the name of Grace Ramsay, contains a passage expressing a similar sentiment. In recounting what took place shortly before the death of this saintly prelate, the writer says, ' And then, seeming quite to forget that any one was present, he broke out into a most beautiful prayer, full of sorrow, love, resignation, and every virtue befitting his state. This lasted for a while, wrote the Bishop of Beverley (Dr. Cornthwaite), and then he turned suddenly to me and said, "There, when I can speak no longer, I mean that." ' Dr. Grant died at Rome whilst attending the Vatican Council, on June 1, 1870.

We do dispraise ourselves for such and such a Superbia. thing, that others may thereby have occasion to commend us.　And this is called a pride ' by hook or by crook.'

Observationes politicæ.

The common people are more easily won by cheap and unprofitable courtesies than by churlish benefits.

Ebrietas.

Sir William Stanley told me on 14 April, 1668, that he had once at Hooton my Lord M—, the three T's, and I think some few more for 3 or 4 nights, and that there were consumed in his house during their stay 16 dozen bottles of wine, 2 hogsheads of beer, and 2 barrels of ale.

Anglicè loquendi modus.

Observe this manner of speaking, viz., 'The thing was done by the King's command,' and thus, ' The thing, no doubt, was done by the King's command.'　The first assertion is positive, the second is doubtful, by reason of the words ' no doubt,' which yet ought rather to confirm the position.　This happened by the long insincere use of that word.　And I fear the same may be said of others.　The nobility at the Coronation, 1661, in making homage to the King, said, they would live and die with him, &c., against all manner of ' folks.'　In the 8th Ed[n] of Claudius Maugre's French Grammar (1678) there is also his short English Grammar, which is very pretty and remarkable to be done by an extern. Yet he doth commit some errors in the matter of pronunciation, which I think proceeds from the great conversation he had at London with ladies and nice things.

We translate the words ' Utinam ' and ' Ave ' into ' Would to God ' and   God save you,' whereas indeed there is no mention of God.   My Protestant Bible englishes ' Ave,' ' God speed.'

We pronounce the   letter *i* variously and different from other nations.   Consider it in China, ditch, &c.   How can it be proper to say ' Chyna,' and yet improper and rustical to say ' dych ' ?


The histories which relate the   rebellious wars    Puritani. of the Puritans against Charles I. are (amongst many others) the 1st and 2nd part of Dr. Bate's history in Latin concerning our late wars.   This Bate   had   been   Cromwell's   physician.   Thomas May was the Parliament's Latin historian, and wrote their history partially.   Baker's Chronicle, or rather the continuation of Baker by Ph, hath very much of that history, but the man that pleases me best for exactness and brevity is

T. Hobbes, who has writ a considerable treatise[1] of 2s. or 3s. price.  The name I remember not.

*Patientia et impatientia.*

Bishop Juxon of Canterbury was a most patient and gentle man.  When he was Bishop of London and Lord Treasurer, a distressed gentlewoman desired him to pay her a good sum of money which was granted her out of the Exchequer.  He told her indeed that he could not do it for want of money in the treasury, but that she should be paid when the first money came in.  Whereupon observing that she began to weep, he excused himself very humbly by the necessary reason abovesaid, for this dilatory answer.  Unto whom the good woman replied, ' Oh, my lord, these are tears of joy.  When I made the same suit to my Lord Weston (your Lordship's predecessor), I received a most harsh denial, and now, by your Lordship's most gentle answer, I am put into assured hope.  Oh, the great difference (said she) that there is in men !'  Mr. Thos. Hawarden told me this July 1st, 1663.

Howell, in his ' Familiar Letters ' (Book ii. letter 25) confirms this narrative.  He says, ' I have

[1] ' Behemoth ' was the title of Hobbes' treatise on the Civil War.

known two Lord High Treasurers of England of quite
contrary humours, one successively after the other ;
the one, though he did the suitor's business, yet he
went murmuring ; and the other, though he did it
not, was used to dismiss the party with some satisfaction.'

Richard Lord Weston, who contrasts here un-
favourably with Archbishop Juxon, was born 1577 ;
sent as Ambassador to Bohemia, 1619 ; Chancellor
of Exchequer, 1621–4 ; Ambassador to Brussels,
1622 ; cr. Baron Weston of Keyland, Essex, 1628 ;
Lord Treasurer of England, 1628 ; cr. Earl of
Portland, 1633 ; ob. Mch. 12, 1635. He married
Frances Waldegrave, and had issue, but the titles
expired with his own family about 1688, at the
death of his son Thomas, who was fourth Earl of
Portland.

A man who showed a dromedary in most Angli.
parts of England told me (1662) that he found
more profit thereby in Lancashire than in any
other county. John Butler the mountebank, born
in Berkshire, told me (July 17, 1663) that he
found nowhere in England more money stirring
among the common people than in Lancashire
He commended for the like plenty, Cheshire,
Suffolk, and Norfolk. He saith that this is a
healthful country, that the moist parts eastward,
especially the Isle of Ely, are the most unhealthful.
That in the moist parts and in the shires that

O

abound with fruits, are the worst teeth : the worst
eyes about the fens : that corns on the feet in
Leicestershire, Northamptonshire, and other dry
countries are contracted by much ploughing.

> Dr. Plot, in his 'Natural History of Staffordshire'
> (published 1686), mentions the burial many years
> before in a field at Tixall, of a dromedary which
> had died through the neglect of its keeper. This
> may not improbably have been the very animal
> which Mr. Blundell saw. The Doctor speculates
> upon the curious surmises that the discovery of the
> bones in after ages may give rise to.

*Justitia
civilis.*

In June 1676 I came from London by coach
with Sergeant Edward Rigby, a Parliament man,
who told me that some years ago it was moved in
the House (and I think it was he who first moved
it) that there should be abatement made of the
excessive fees in courts, and thereupon a committee was appointed to consider of it, of which
he was the chairman. It proceeded far in the
matter, and he brought their report concerning the
same to the House. After waiting ten days at the
bar to deliver the same, the House being busy
about a Bill for raising two millions to maintain
the war against the Dutch, he could not be admitted, whereupon he told the Speaker, that the

matter which he had there to present would advantage the generality of the people of England more than the value of that whole sum, and I think he said that the advantage would be made in as short a time as while the said money was raising. However, he was never admitted to present the report, and he told me he did believe that the men of law in the House, foreseeing their own damage thereby, did hinder the whole matter.

Mr. John Entwistle, the lawyer, held in my hearing, in August 1676, that Mr. Pemberton having received 30*l.* to draw a release (or general release), called it ' Porter's wages.'

> Edward Rigby, serjeant-at-law, born 1627, was third son of Colonel Alexander Rigby, and was M.P. for Preston 1661–1678–9, and again re-elected for the subsequent session.—J. E. B.

I did once inquire of a haberdasher of hats, who had a wholesale trade with most parts of England, whether he had observed that any counties of England did produce heads remarkably great or remarkably little ; and he told me that the heads of Lincolnshire men were generally smaller than any others that he met with.

The most universal detraction proceeds from

*Anglia.*

*Detractio.*

State policy.    In the reign of Queen Elizabeth, our English books were full of all manner of disgraceful things concerning the Spaniard, because he was then our enemy.    Since then, we have stood in fear of the French; at least, we have envied their greatness, and slandered them accordingly.    In our late wars with Holland, one Downing, who had been (as I take it) the King's agent or ambassador there, printed a book (which I have in my library) against the Dutch, charging them bitterly with many foul things, and saying to this effect, that they have cost more coin and Christian blood to Europe than it hath spent and lost by all the wars it has had with the great Turk.    In that speech of the Earl of Shaftesbury, spoken in the Parliament about March 1678–9, which was thought to have occasioned the murder of the Bishop of St. Andrews, and the rebellion in Scotland, he was most severe against the Government of that kingdom.    He speaks as if the arbitrary power thereof did quite exceed the tyranny used in those which we do esteem the eastward and southern kingdoms of the world.    Note the scornful habit of detraction which the English for sundry ages have used against the Welsh and the Scots.

This vice is not peculiar to England, yet we have seen here its dismal effects, especially since the revelations made by Dr. Oates in 1678. Mons. Rob, in his history (written in French) shows how the persecution of the Christians in Japan was grounded upon a malicious lie forged by the Dutch for their own advantage, to discountenance the trade of the Catholic European merchants. The consequence of this persecution, I fear, hath been the destruction of all visible Christianity in Japan. By God's just judgment, the chief author of that contrivance had a punishment even in this world most exemplary strange.

I have heard of one Mr. Fielding, a forward Duellum. duellist, who notwithstanding did most shamefully misbehave himself (I mean most like a coward) in one of our great battles in the late Dutch war, at sea. And this day, January 29, 1667, my cousin, Margaret Molyneux (who, having waited sundry years upon Madam Eliot, at London, had occasion to know the truth of many such things), told me, for certain, that the said Fielding, coming out of a tavern in London, with his own brother, some months ago, called to a coachman for a coach. The fellow not being willing to take him in, he was so incensed that, drawing his sword, and being hindered by his said brother from hurting the coachman, he presently killed his brother without more ado, and was fairly hanged for his pains.

My good friend, Mr. Da. Sa. (whom I call son) told me this following story, this present May 12, 1668. Mr. Grosvenor, son of Sir Richard Grosvenor, who was killed some time since, said to Mrs. Houghton (now widow of Mr. Gilbert Houghton) that day before he was killed, that if any man was to ride near his footman (who, I think, was to run a race that day), he would kill him, or be killed by him. Mr. D. S. told me that Mrs. Houghton told him this. But the conclusion was this—Mr. Grosvenor that day switched Mr. Roberts, and drew upon him ; but Mr. Roberts killed him with his sword, and before he died, he said it was his own fault.

*Longevi.* It was ridiculous in the beggar (100 years old and odd) who, to move charity, said he was a poor motherless and fatherless creature.

*Judicia in Catholicorum hostes.* Mr. Howell in 9 letter, sec. 5, says, 'I never heard of anything that prospered which, being once designed for the honour of God, was alienated from that use.'

A cross was pulled down at Tewkesbury by the prevailing power of a Puritan minister, long before the general ruin of crosses through England. An inferior townsman of the same sect made use of one the stones of this cross for walling about his well, and some of them (wherein had been pictures of Our Lady and St. John) were converted into swine troughs. The event was this: His wife and sundry of his children became blind, and he drowned himself in the same well. Narravit mihi Dnus. Thos. Stanton, qui degens tunc temporis in illo oppido, cum erat admodum juvenis, non semel viderat hominem, qui postea (ut dictum est) sacrilegio suo fatum accelerasset.[1]

It was proved at Hugh Peter's arraignment that he had said in his sermon that Charing Cross had made more Papists, and done more harm in that way, than any pulpit in London had done good. He was hanged at this place.

---

[1] This was told me by the Rev. Thos. Stanton, who when a youth resided at that period in the town, and had more than once seen the man who afterwards, as it was said, hastened his death by his sacrilege.

Longevi.

I saw Thomas Parr's picture at full length among Cardinal Mazarine's rarities in his Palace at Paris, 1660. In the same year, as I travelled betwixt Antwerp and Breda, I found posted upon the wall of a poor inn the picture of Anthony Haasethus, who was Primus Pastor Gulensis in the Diocese of Liege, where he lived the parson of the parish 100 years together. He died, aged 125, A.D. 1586. Being asked by the Bishop of Liege what means he had taken to prolong his life, he answered that he had always abstained from three things, ' women, wine, and anger.' This I have transcribed out of the Latin subscription at the bottom of the same picture, which picture I bought, and have it now in my house.

Straffordiæ
Comes.

The King said to the Parliament that the misdemeanours of the Earl of Strafford were so great and many, that he was not fit to serve the place of a Constable. Yet there is no question but these expressions did not proceed from any just will in the King, but only to have saved his life. The loss of this (by his Majesty's consent) did wonderfully afflict and scruple the King; as appeareth by the sad expression he used to the Earl of Carnwath, from whom I received it.

I saw the Earl of Strafford in Dublin (June 1639), when he was then Lord Deputy, in far greater state (in some respects) than the King of England. The Earl of Ormond (now Marquis) was pointed out to me riding in the Deputy's own troop. I saw one princely stable of the Deputy's, wherein I judged the worst of 60 horses for the great saddle to be worth 30*l.* He was an excellent orator, as appears by his speeches at the bar ; and a passing wise man. A Colonel of Parliament told me that beyond the seas it is reported of England that it produceth but one wise man in an age, and that the people gaze on him awhile as a monster, then cut off his head. 'So,' said he, 'did they do by Sir Thomas More and the Earl of Strafford.' This story I was telling to the present Earl, his son, who told me (September 1659) that the King of Sweden's Embassador at London did very lately procure there for his master (by his especial command) the pictures of these very same two wise persons I mentioned. His Lordship told me further, that his Lordship's paternal estate was 4 to 5,000*l.* per annum, which he lived to double, but dying in about 80,000*l.* debt, he himself had sold (one-

P

fifth part too cheap) about a moiety of the said estate to pay the aforesaid debts.    20,000*l.* of this debt was incurred by being surety for the King, or by taking up the like sum for his Majesty, at the beginning of the war in Yorkshire.

The Earl of Strafford, upon the scaffold, left as a prime precept to his son, that he should not meddle with Church lands, for they would prove a canker to his estate.

The sad expression which the King made use of to the Earl of Carnwath respecting Strafford is not recorded, but it resembled, no doubt, his utterances on the scaffold.  Clarendon seems to attribute to this Earl the loss of the Battle of Naseby.  He says that when the King was on the point of charging the enemy, the Earl of Carnwath, who rode next to him, on a sudden laid his hand on the King's bridle, and swearing two or three full-mouthed Scotch oaths, said, 'Will you go upon your death in an instant?' and, before his Majesty understood what he was about, turned his horse round.  His followers seeing the movement fled in disorder.  ('Hist. Rebell.,' vol. ii. p. 508.)  Mr. Blundell would probably meet the second Earl of Strafford at Knowsley, as this nobleman had married Henrietta, daughter of James, Earl of Derby.

*Aucupium.*    The use of stalking-horses is great and notably advantageous in some parts.  Horses are easily taught.  Some do use to have a painted horse carried upon a frame. But, doubtless, a bust is more easy and not less useful. I know some to have stalked so near to partridges that the birds have pecked at the horses' legs. Let your painted horse or cow have one side of a different colour to the other.

Dotterells in Lincolnshire are taken by candle-light ; for whilst they imitate the fowler's gestures, they suffer him to cast his net upon them.

Our posterity will hardly believe the extrava- Pecunia vitiata.
gance and damage which we find now in England by the clipping of our silver coin. The present Tuesday, January 11, 1695, I received from my servant Walter Thelwall (who writes this affair after my dictate, and knows the same to be true) the just sum of 10*l.* 18*s.* for cattle of mine which he sold yesterday at Newbrough fair. Out of this sum I picked out thirteen of the smallest clipt shillings. These thirteen shillings being laid on a pair of scales which were used for the weighing of gold, were then clearly overweighted by five broad shillings chosen at adventure, viz. by two Eliza-beth shillings and three shillings of Charles I., and I found that these five shillings weighed just one

P 2

ounce.   However, when I had put the thirteen
shillings abovesaid to the rest of the same, and
weighed altogether the foresaid sum of 10*l.* 18*s.*,
I found the whole weight to be very near 26 ounces,
and by throwing in an old ninepence it clearly
turned the scales.   Now, according to this account
the said 10*l.* 18*s.*, which ought to have weighed
43⅗ ounces, was no more but 26 ounces, bating an
old ninepence.

Sanguinis<br/>emissio.

My landlord at La Fleche, Julian Bionteau,
writ and printed a book (which book I have)
against the common practice of the doctors at
Paris in taking too much blood from their patients.
He speaks of horrid abuses in that, and doth
bitterly condemn it.   He entitles himself the
King's physician.

> Howell, in his 'Familiar Letters' (Book I. Letter
> 21), refers to this Parisian custom of blood-letting.
> As the date of this letter is 1622, it would appear
> that the practice had not abated sixty years later,
> when Mr. Blundell was at La Fleche :—
> 'At first they let me blood, and I parted with
> above 50 ounces in less than a fortnight ; for phle-
> botomy is so much practised here, that if one's little
> finger ache they presently open a vein : and to
> balance the blood on both sides, they usually let
> blood on both arms.'

Catholics deny the oath, yet keep their alle- Apparatus de Catholicis
giance to the King.   Others take the oath and fail Anglicanis.
in allegiance.   Mr. Blood was an Irish Protestant,
and so great a rebel or plotter, that a great sum (I
think 500*l.* at the least) was promised by proclamation to those that could apprehend him.   This man
did afterwards steal the King's crown in the Tower
of London, and was taken in the fact; yet for some
supposed discoveries by him made of other traitors,
he had his liberty, and, as was said, the King's
favour, so that he frequently walked in the court
at Whitehall.   It may seem that some treasons are
too great to be punished, as some services are too
great to be requited.   There is a great difference
between the case of the Pendrells, who being Catholics cannot appear in the court, though they
saved the King's life with the hazard of their own,
and the case of notorious traitors (*olim*) who are
now in favour.   Popery is an odd religion.   If I
mistake not, the proclamation against Blood was
in the year 1666, and he stole the crown about
three or four years after.   His brother-in-law,
Lachy, was hanged for rebellion in Ireland.   He
was a Minister.

Mr. Blundell was not singular in his surprise at

the favour experienced by the notorious Colonel
Blood. Sir R. Burgoyne, writing to Sir Nathaniel
Hobarts, February 12, 1671–2, says, 'A fortnight
since my Lord Brook told me that Blood had not
only his own pardon for all his villainy, but also had
procured the like for Desburrough, Kelsey, &c. :
certainly, some designs more than ordinary are on
foot, that such persons are received into favour.'—
(Historical Commissioners' 7th Report, Appendix.)

*Justitia
civilis.*

Sir Josias Child, in his discourse of trade,
printed in octavo, 1693, assigns one reason of the
prosperity of the Hollanders to be their fair dealing
in packing up their goods, as herrings, codfish, &c.,
and ascribes the disrepute and loss to the English
by taking the contrary course.

*Plays.*

Prologue to a stage play, which I made at the
entreaty of some country neighbours who were to
act the play—about Christmas 1647 :

The bitter storms of war are over-blown,
And joyful peace succeedeth in the place,
The husbandman may now enjoy his own,
And look the armèd soldier in the face.
The soldier too doth live an honest life,
Confines himself to quarter and his pay ;
And each one, weary with the bloody strife,
Hath sheathed his sword, and now begins to play.
And to a PLAY we do invite you all,
According to the custom of the time ;

Though in that art our talent be but small,
Our best endeavours cannot prove a crime.
Excuse us then, who, with a willing heart,
Have ta'en some pains to entertain you here,
And shall we hope (if no man miss his part),
Give cause to think you have not bought it dear.
Then patient sit, with silence, three short hours,
And if you like not then, the fault is ours.
*Non omnes arbusta juvent.*

Bare the roots of your trees and make a hole in a principal root, and then put in a pretty quantity of powder, made of such things as you desire your apple should taste of; as of cloves, mace, nutmeg, or such like.

*To impart flavour to fruit.*

Quære—if it will not work that effect in other fruit trees, and whether the bole of the tree will not serve to put it in, or whether the bole must be cloven or bored.

Sir George Blundell of Edenderry, King's County, Ireland, Bart. His estate is esteemed to be 1,000*l.* per annum. He told me (1662) that he was descended from Blundell of Ince, and that he gives the same coat with a half-moon.

*Blundellio-rum familiæ.*

He told me likewise then of one Sir George Blundell of Cardington in Bedfordshire, then lately knighted. The Earl of Aylesbury told me in 1676 that Sir George Blundell was then a D.L. in that county.

There is a Baron of this name, Blundell, living about a mile from Douay, of whom I have often heard as a person exceedingly remarkable for valour in war. I found in the French Heraldry three different families of this name in France, besides an advocate whom I knew at Rouen, A.D. 1660. They are all of different families, and their coat armour is not the same with ours. Yet Mr. Thomas Massey told me that he saw a coach in Paris on which were our arms, and that an attendant told him the master's name was Blundell.

The Blundells of Cardington were descended from Thomas, a younger son of William Blundell of Ince Blundell, Esq., who was living 1534. Sir George Blundell, Knt., of this race, married Elizabeth, daughter and heiress of John Gascoigne, Esq., of Cardington, Beds. He was killed at the Isle of Rhe, in 1630, and had received in the early part of that century a grant of land, subsequently called Blundell, in King's County, Ireland. His brother Sir Francis, Secretary of Affairs in Ireland, 1619, was created a Bart. in the following year. Sir Montague Blundell, fourth Bart., was advanced in 1720 to the dignities of Baron Edenderry and Viscount Blundell, but through default of male issue, these titles expired in 1756. The Sir George Blundell spoken of as a

D.L., lies buried at Cardington, and the inscription on his monument is a curious bit of Latinity. It commences thus : 'Hic jacet corpus Georgii Blundell Militis, Directi successoris et Hæredis Blundellianæ et Gasconianæ familiæ Bedfordiensis. Obiit Nov. 11, 1688.'

There are two or three families still flourishing in France who bear the name and arms of Blondell.

My neighbour Richard Johnson told me this day (August 18, 1665), in plain terms, that those of his religion did not use baptism by water at all ; and that it is not lawful for them to fight in any case ; and that one Bennet, in Derbyshire, first called them Quakers. Quakers.

Mrs. Trask was a kind of primitive Quaker, yet was she called a Sabbatarian. She lived in prison (where she died) a most strict penitential life fifteen years.

One John Blaket (if I mistake not the name) is a great man among the Quakers, and liveth near Sedbergh in Yorkshire.

'This was Justice Bennet of Derby, who was the first that called us Quakers, because I bid them tremble at the word of the Lord.' This was in the year 1650.—(George Fox's Journal, ed. Leeds, 1836, vol. i. p. 132.) Fox's committal for six months to Derby Gaol in 1649 was signed by Gervas Bennet, J.P.—J. E. B.

Commoda
reipublicæ
optanda.

It were good that all casual manslaughters, as well as murders and executions of felons, were yearly printed in England, upon which many observations might be made of singular use. The Coroner and Clerk of the Crown might much concur to the doing of this.

This summer (1669), a man was overwhelmed with earth in a sandhill at the Grange whilst he was seeking to take rabbits out of a hole ; and quickly after, another man perished in Male (but 3 miles off), just in the same manner, in a sandy cop. This I think had hardly happened if he had heard of the other man's chance.

Let there likewise be a history of all trials of felons and duellists, &c., even when the offender comes off with life. But this, alas! would rather encourage offenders by the slack execution of justice.

Honesty is wanting in England, and that want corrupts all commodities and stops the well proceeding of all affairs. Mr. Thomas Clayton, Merchant, told me about the year 1672, when we had war with Holland, that even then he would rather trust Hollanders than Englishmen to negotiate by way of factorage his affairs abroad.

It were good to have steps or seats (as in a cock-pit), for the better sight of public executions and trials, as at Tyburn, Westminster Hall, &c.

In April 1669, Mr. Edward Lloyd told me *Arbores ingentiores.* that his father Mr. Robert Lloyd of Place-ys-asaudd, in Denbighshire (not far from Wrexham), had a tree growing near his house which was seven fathom (measuring by men's arms) round about the bole, which bole was seven yards high to the first bough. But when I seemed not to credit this, he did seriously affirm that he had been assured that it was either five or seven fathom in compass, but that indeed he had never measured it.

In Lent, which was in the year 1648–9, just *Moon out of order.* about the equinox, there was a report of the moon rising at an unusual time, and it went a higher or longer course than ordinary. This, they say, was observed by the market men and fishermen, which I little regarded ; but one Sunday, when I was at dinner, some one bringing word that the moon appeared out of course, I went down into the orchard, and it being then an exceeding clear day, about 12 o'clock or before, I saw the moon about an hour

Q 2

and a half high to my judgment, and shining with a
perfect orb in the east, if I be not mistaken, or
rather one point toward the south.   That evening
about seven o'clock we went down to the back porch,
where standing still, we saw the moon in a full
clear orb over the chapel chamber chimney or
thereabouts.   It appeared higher to our judgment
than ever we had seen the sun in the longest day.
My cousin Heaton was with me then, and at noon
my brother Haggerston.   It was observed to go
such a like strange course a day or two after.   If
I be not much mistaken, some did affirm (with
such testimony as I then believed it), that the
moon was up at least 21 hours together.   However, I think the prodigy was very remarkable and
the greatest that ever I saw.

The editor has been favoured by the Rev. Syl-
vester J. Hunter, S.J., with the following observations on this phenomenon :—' If my astronomy is
not at fault, I suspect that the phenomenon was akin
to that of the harvest moon, which commonly does
not attract the same attention at the spring equinox
as in the autumn.   The harvest moon is much
more noticeable in some years than in others, and a
rough calculation that I have made seems to show,
that 1648–9 would be one of the years in which it
would be most prominent.   In these same years the
moon, when in the north, would attain a greater

height than that of the sun in the longest day, by
about five degrees, or ten times her own diameter.
And in this we have a remarkable proof of the ac-
curacy of the observations, made as they were by
the naked eye. As to the moon being up 21 hours
he speaks doubtfully, and with reason : if I am not
mistaken, she never can be up for much more than
18 hours in Lancashire. The longest stay above
the horizon will occur just in the same year as that
in which she attains the greatest light in the heavens,
and rises most nearly at the same time for several
successive nights.'

A prologue to a sword dance, spoken at Lathom
upon Ash Wednesday, 1638 :

The common proverb teacheth us to say,
'Tis hazardous with sharp-edged tools to play.
Yet we t' increase your honour's pleasures shall,
Adding more triumph to this carnival,
Forget the Muses' Hill, those nymphs, those dames,
And practise with our swords th' Olympic games.
Be but auspicious to our play, while we
This night shall Mars prefer to Mercury.

Mr. Blundell, although already married, was not
more than eighteen years of age at this time, and,
as he himself confesses, remarkably fond of all
youthful amusements. Lathom House, the ancient
seat of the Earls of Derby, was then in its glory,
soon, alas ! to be reduced, by miserable civil broils,
to a shapeless ruin. It was the scene of the well-
known and memorable defence made by the spirited
Countess Charlotte de la Tremouille, who frequently
entertained our Cavalier in after years at Knowsley.

Condæus
Princeps.

The present prince (1659) was born Sept. 8, 1621, and is a most bold and vigilant soldier, but immoderate (as they say) in his amours. He sleepeth no more commonly but three hours in the night, and useth to say that the devil rocketh him that sleepeth longer. *Narravit mihi* Gul. Clifton, Feb. 8, 1659.

Dracon

I do not know in what part of the world dragons are now to be found, nor do I know their shape or size.

This rivals the remarkable chapter on snakes in the 'History of Iceland from the Danish of Horrebow,' which is referred to in Boswell's 'Life of Johnson.'

Carmen.

Tu pacata vale rore lavata caput.

This verse is the same read backwards. It was made by occasion of a woman dispossessed of the devil by baptism.

Vulnera
graviora
sanata.

Sir Ferdinand Carey, a huge corpulent knight, was shot through his body ; the bullet entering at the navel and coming out at his back, killed his man behind him, yet he liveth still and is like to recover.—Mr. Howell's letter, 32, sec. 3. Yet he hath it from a second hand.

A servant maid, at the siege of Hardin (Harwarden) Castle, was shot in the mouth, and the bullet came out of her fundament, and she recovered the hurt. She served Sir William Neale, who affirmed this to be true in my hearing. But the bullet (you must know) came, many days after it was shot, through the common passage.

Choose rather to lend money to your friend (though you borrow it yourself) even upon his single bond, than to enter into bond with him.

*Præcepta olitica.*

There are five Colleges of the Society in England :

*Jesu Societa Anglicana.*

1. St. Ignatius's College at London, wherein they say are such of the novices as are to be trained in England.

2. St. Peter and Paul's College at Norwich.

3. St. Xavier's College in North Wales.

4. The College of the Holy Conception in Derbyshire, Leicester, and thereabouts. This college was esteemed the richest of all the foundation thereof, having been no less than 7,000*l.* and the

yearly revenue thence arising 625*l.* But 6,100*l.* of that foundation is in great danger to be lost in ill hands. A.D. 1660.

5. The College of Bd. Aloysius, including Lancashire, Cheshire, Staffordshire, and no more.

Besides the colleges there are many parts of England called ' Residences,' not belonging to the colleges, as Yorkshire, Cornwall, Northumberland, &c. In 1660 there were 23 fathers in the College of St. Aloysius. About Michaelmas 1663, Father Courtney the Provincial came into Lancashire, and received an account or list of 2,500 penitents under those of his order. *Narravit mihi* Ds. Peter Bradshaigh.

> Father Edward Courtney, whose real name was Leedes, was the son of Sir Thomas Leedes of Wappingthorne, in Sussex, and had a brother Thomas, likewise of the Society of Jesus. Edward, born 1599, became a student at the English College, Rome, 1618, and entered the novitiate S.J. on August 28, 1621. After his ordination he was employed in various capacities, and must have had a talent for government, as before his death he filled nearly every office in his Province. He was English Provincial, 1660–4, and ended his days at St. Omer's College on October 3, 1677. (Foley's ' Records,' S.J., vol. i. p. 251.)
>
> Rev. Peter Bradshaigh was one of three brothers,

uncles of Mr. Blundell, who embraced the Society of Jesus. He died April 17, 1676, aged 66.

It is very remarkable that the English in this age have no great talent in writing Latin prose. See my history of the expedition into the Isle of Rhe, writ most pitifully by an English Lord. But that which passes all for barbarous Latin is the work of the *classical* divines, mentioned at large in the history of Presbitery. *Latinè scribendi modus.*

> The author of the former work was Edward Lord Herbert of Cherbury, of whom Anthony A. Wood writes (vol. iii. 240): 'Under the tuition of an eminent tutor [he] laid the foundation of that admirable learning whereof he was afterwards a compleat master. The book is entitled, 'Expeditio in Ream Insulam,' Authore Edovardo Domino Herbert, Barone de Cherbury in Anglia. . . . Anno MDCXXX. Quam Publici Juris fecit Timotheus Balduinus, LSD. e Coll. Omn. Anim. Apud Oxon. Socius. Lond. 8vo. 1656.—J. E. B.

It was the saying of Sir Thomas Tildesley (as his lady told me), that he would follow his business close, to the end that he might the more enjoy his pleasures. Œconomia.

I spent in France a great part of the years Festi dies.

R

1680 and 1681, and there I found that our catalogue of the new holydays was not then observed ;
yet sundry days of Saints whose names we scarce
know are kept holy there in particular dioceses.

If there be four million of working people in a
country who are each able to earn 6*d.* per diem, the
work of one day will amount to 100,000*l.*   So that
the difference of working and not working of the
people of a whole nation is no small matter as to
civil and political respects.   Note the different
consequence of industry and idleness by compar-
ing the present state of France, Holland, Flanders,
&c., with the present state of Spain and the lazy
old Irish.   A thousand weighty matters may be
considered pro and con. on this occasion.

A.D. 1683.   Christmas began on Tuesday, so
that we had at that time eight holydays altogether,
Sunday being included therein.   Immediately before that Christmas, we had six days beginning on
Wednesday 19th, whereof five were fasting-days,
one holyday, and one Sunday ; so that there were
at that time fourteen days altogether, which were
all of them either holydays or fasting-days.   Note
that Friday 21st (St. Thomas the Apostle) was not
only holyday but double fasting-day, to say nothing

of the Friday and Saturday following, which were days of abstinence. I was at Paris in July 1680, and found there that the 26th of that month (St. Anne's day) was not kept holyday, neither was the 24th kept as a vigil either by fasting or abstinence. At La Fleche, in Rogation week, I found there was abstinence for five days, but no days fasted, whereas we fast two days in England.

> The want of regular Church government in Mr. Blundell's time long prevented any change in these matters ; but the fasting-days in England have since been much reduced in number, and are no longer burdensome.

In hac domo quam a vermiculis mutuo accepi, cum fratribus meis, sub spe resurrectionis ad vitam, jaceo Samuel, permissione divinâ Episcopus hujus Insulæ.

*Rutteri Epitaphium.*

> Siste lector,
> Vide et ride
> Palatium Episcopi.

This epitaph was given to me June 18, 1662, by Monsieur Daniel Trioche, Secretary to the Countess of Derby, who saith that it was sent out of the Isle of Man, and that it was found among the Bishop's papers.

> This inscription was on a plate in St. German's

Cathedral, Isle of Man, but was stolen by a tourist, before 1825.—J. E. B.

Ocreæ un- A pint of ale, a halfpenny in wax, fresh butter
gendæ. one quarter ; melt them together.   Afterwards (but not before, lest it flame), add some turpentine. And so use it.   I had this from a shoemaker in Chester, a Quaker.   Try it on the boots of your servant.   When boots are new, fill them with strong wort and tanners' bark bruised.   Hang them up for two or three months till all be dried in ; then oil them as you please for softness.   This (saith Major Gibson) is the best way.

Anomola. Now in my old age (ætatis 59), having spent much time in study for the knowledge of things, I find, with great regret, that I know not so much as what is meant by the common names of things that are most commonly known and spoken of. And I do persuade myself that the most part of our disputes were ended, if our words were always such as clearly to express our thoughts.   How little do Protestants know what we mean by our Church's *infallibility, indulgences* for sin, or *merit* for good works !   But let us take more familiar notions : a *day*, a *month*, a *year.*   I find in Miege's

French Dictionary this which follows : — ' Les Babiloniens commencoient le jour au lever du soleil, les Juifs et les Atheniens le commencoient au coucher, et les Italiens les imitent. Les Egyptiens le commencoient à midi.' As for the beginning, the end, and the just term of a year, the differences in sundry ages and places have been unspeakably great, and caused great confusion.

The most weighty controversy that happened in my time in England before the Judges, was to determine the meaning of the words *twelve months.* The innocent Irishmen had only twelve months allowed them by Act of Parliament to be restored to their lands, after which there was to be no restoration. Upon this, the Court of Claims at Dublin sat one whole year, and making a quick despatch near the end of that term, some hundreds of persons were in the last month of the year restored to their lands. Whereupon their adversaries got the matter to be heard in England, pretending that twelve lunar months was the time allowed. But, contrary to men's expectation, the cause was carried by the Irish.

*Exempli gratiâ* : if a man desire to measure <sup>Computandi ratio.</sup>

the length of a field or way by pacing over the same, and he finds it hard to remember the several scores or twenties, so that he will drop a pebble into his pocket at the end of each score ; which being tedious may be helped by keeping time to the motion of your feet with these or the like words, viz.—

Who saw Jack Straw—one.

Who saw Jack Straw—two, &c.

Which being continued to twenty, the whole number is 100.

So one may count at shuttle cock, either with the same words or thus—

Take care, strike fair—one ;

or one may say

Take care, strike fair, pit pat, hit that—one ;

which being repeated to twenty, makes just nine score.

This thing may be sundry other ways improved to serious uses, notwithstanding the matter may seem to be ridiculous.

Mensura li-
quidorum.

An old wine-tierce which, being filled with claret, I had formerly bought, was, when I had drawn it out, measured (*me vidente*) with water.

It was filled with 131 size—quarts. I mean such quarts, 32 whereof make a Winchester bushel. The quart which I used therein had been measured by my servant James Hoghton with the brazen standard quart at Liverpoole, about the year 1676.

Many persons have money which they desire to put out for lawful interest, &c. ; but they are wholly ignorant of the means to do it. Many others would take up money in extreme necessity, and are willing to give security ; but they know not where to find money. This hath been the reason the scriveners of London have been employed as brokers for money, with benefit to themselves and commodity to the borrower and lender. This might be practised with much advantage to the country, in each county of England, by the means of some discreet honest person in each town of note, whose known employment it should be either to put out money and take security, or at least to be able to give the names of the borrowers and lenders of such sums as are required to be borrowed and lent. This was the judgment of Mr. T. Sel.

The above was writ about the year 1659, since when great practice hath been made in this kind

*Commoda Reipublicæ optanda.*

*Brokers for money :*

within our neighbourhood, so that now, this present year 1683, it seems so convenient to borrowers and lenders, that I think it is like to continue.

And I believe the like might be practised with great advantage to the country, in other and for Land and Marriages; matters : as in buying and selling of land, and even in marriages (if the person employed be discreet and tender of other men's credits). In these he might be used (if you please), no otherwise than as an informer or intelligencer betwixt the parties, and his commission might be so restrained as that he should only tell the circumstances—as the value, price, site, and buildings upon the land : the age, portion, quality, beauty, &c., of such a maid or widow ; and the like of such a bachelor or widower as desireth to have a wife. And when he findeth that these informations are agreeable to the inquirer's desires, he may inform the parties concerned ; and telling withal the several qualities of the inquirer, if they do then seem to be grateful to the other, he may name each party to the other, and so leave them to transact their business. This course seemeth to prevent two extremes : the one of wanting the commodity of the thing you desire, by a bashful silence, and the other of becoming necessarily the common chat of the neighbourhood, if you should after publish your desire to buy or sell land, to marry, or the like.

Some such way might be used for the hiring of servants or 'prentices, and for the utterance of divers wares and commodities.

*and Servants, &c.*

It would be very expedient if each parish or village might have some place, as the church, smithy, wherein to publish (by papers posted up) the wants either of the buyer or seller, as, such a field to be let, such a servant or such a service to be had, &c. And it seemeth convenient that each man that will sell his horse should tie a mark or sign thereof in the bridle. For, in regard it is often ill taken to ask a gentleman the price of his horse, many necessary bargains are hindered ; as likewise, if a man should now declare his willingness to sell his horse, it would argue some hidden fault, whereas in so general a usage it were not so like to be suspected.

*Things to be sold, &c.*

There was a book published at London weekly about the year 1657, which was called (as I remember) 'The Publick Advice.' It gave information in very many of these particulars. Quære—-if it continues still to do so, or the reason that it doth not.

A.D. 1660.—There is an office near the Old Exchange in London, called the office of ‘ Publick Advice.’ From thence both printed and private informations of this useful nature are always to be had. But what they print is no more than a leaf or less in a diurnal. I was in this office. The diurnal consisted of sixteen pages quarto in 1689.

*Considera-*
*tiones piæ.*
I am convinced by reason and my own experience (to say nothing of faith), that it is extreme folly to be transported either with joy or grief in temporal respects. That which hath an end is nothing, saith a great Saint. However, it would seem something if it would last some number of years. But we do see desperate and griping sorrows tread upon the heels of the greatest joys. The very day (to the best of my memory and observation) of my own greatest joy did immediately precede the day (in all appearance and probability) of my greatest loss and grief. Yet, notwithstanding that this loss was no less than my whole estate by incurring delinquency and the mutilation of the strongest limb in my body by a musket shot, it hath proved in the end (as far as human prudence can yet conjecture) the greatest

temporal fortune that ever befell me, and that for many reasons, partly known to others, but principally to myself. These changes are no wonder, when we know of far greater happening to whole cities. To-day the bells and the bonfires express the violent passions of an overjoyed people, when to-morrow their own reeking blood must extinguish their flaming buildings. That thing for which we do most labour and pray, and for the happening whereof we are even transported with joy, is not seldom our utter destruction, and that speedily.

1665, May.—Richard Airey, of London, his bill Tailors' bills. for Mall [Mary, Mr. Blundell's daughter] :—

| | | | |
|---|---|---|---|
| For a sky-coloured silk mohair coat . | £2 | 17 | 0 |
| „ „ coloured stuff coat bought for her | 1 | 3 | 0 |
| „ „ sky-coloured silk mohair waistcoat | 0 | 17 | 0 |
| „ „ mixed pink-coloured petticoat of | | | |
| good sarcenet . . . . | 1 | 1 | 0 |
| „ „ suit of knots of pink and silver | | | |
| riband . . . . . | 0 | 4 | 6 |
| „ 2 laces . . . . . . | 0 | 0 | 6 |
| | £6 | 3 | 0 |

He speaks also of paying 2*l*. 5*s*. for two hats of equal price, and 1*l*. 8*s*. for a border of hair. Mr.

Airey, on the other hand, had sold for him twenty-seven dozen rabbit skins at 4s. 2d. per dozen, coming to 5l. 12s. 6d.

I paid many round sums for clothes for my son Butler (Richard, afterwards Viscount Mountgarret, who had married, in 1661, Mr. Blundell's daughter Emilia). I do remember particularly a stuff suit and coat when he came to me about April 1661—

| | | | | | |
|---|---|---|---|---|---|
| This I take cost about | . | . | . | .£4 | 5 | 0 |
| His wedding suit and coat of Spanish cloth, being 2 pair of breeches besides the doublet and the coat, cost about | . | 7 | 15 | 0 |
| A velvet coat bought at London, cost | . | 8 | 0 | 0 |
| A hat when he was at London 1661 | . | 1 | 2 | 0 |
| A sword at the same time, about | . | . | 1 | 0 | 0 |

Besides sundry other things, which partly I do not remember, and partly do forbear to put down.

Servants' wages.

1667, May.—It is agreed betwixt me and John Tildesley that he shall serve me one whole year, from May 2, 1667, for 4l. wages, and for such vails as shall happen in the service; but I am not obliged to give him any further reward for his services, either by old clothes or any other way. (Signed by W. Blundell and John Tildesley.)

Upon the eve (December 7) of the Conception of our Lady, I, being of the sodality with others of my family, proposed to our spiritual director that we might all together say the Rosary upon the said feast day. He said he did very well like it, but could not conveniently be present himself, having but weak health and finding that such exercises did spend him. I told him that he might in such a number of persons answer in silence, and no notice would be taken of it. But he said that he found that even the noise of others speaking was often troublesome to him. In fine, we said the Rosary on the said feast day, and although we had not his company, yet he spent the most part of the afternoon of that holyday in playing at tables and shovel-board in the dining-room and in the hall, and at four of the clock and a half retired to his chamber. This gentleman was a person of singular virtue and prudence, and one whom I should have chosen before thousands, as well for a companion as for a director. And this I note that I may remember not to have a bitter prejudice against the actions of such men as I like not, when those whom I like so well will do things so contrary to my judgment.

Mirabilia quædam ad fidem spectantia.

The chaplain whose conduct on this occasion excited the momentary displeasure of Mr. Blundell was, no doubt, the Rev. Francis Waldegrave, S. J. We have already spoken of him in the introductory chapters, and have mentioned the great esteem in which he was held by his patron, who indeed confirms this estimate of him in the foregoing remarks.

The Rosary is still a favourite devotion of the Catholic Church, and sodalities for the daily recital of it have numerous associates. Tables is the same as backgammon, but shovel-board is no longer known as it was formerly played. It seems to have been the forerunner of billiards. An old shovel-board is said to exist at Chartley Hall. It is 31 feet 1 inch long, made up of 260 pieces, 12 or 18 inches long, laid on longer boards underneath, and well jointed. Those who have made a long sea voyage will be familiar with a description of shovel-board played on deck, which is one of the few diversions possible under such conditions. Flat discs of wood are used, and these are propelled with long-handled spades of corresponding size into divisions chalked out at a suitable distance. On the latter are marked the numerals up to 10, with two forfeits of 10, one at each end. The chief amusement seems to consist in driving your enemy out of the winning numbers and lodging yourself in his place. This is varied by dexterous attempts to land him in the forfeits, and to cover skilfully the approaches, that he may not be afterwards relieved.

*Versiones Anglicanæ.*

It is wonderful to see how notably our countrymen do translate anything out of the Latin, either verse or prose, and yet we shall never meet with an Englishman that either writes or speaks Latin commendably.

Sands' translation of Ovid's 'Metamorphoses' is said to bear the bell for a translation in verse. Virgil's 'Æneid' hath ever been esteemed a piece too high to be dealt with, with any hope of success in that kind. Yet hath Ogleby (a fellow that kept a tap house) engaged upon it, and performed it with good applause. May hath done 'Lucan' rarely well, and Virgil's 'Georgics.'

Sir Humphrey Stapleton [? Robert] hath hit very right of the jog of an English style in his version of 'Strada,' yet in sundry places he mistakes the sense of the author. Winterton hath made a most proper piece of English of Drexelius' 'Nine Considerations upon Eternity.' But his different opinions in religion hath made him often to mince and conceal the author's sense.

A good lady of my acquaintance was so curious in her attire, as to send out of Lancashire to London her linen to be washed and starched as often as they were fouled ; such fine linens, I mean, as were used about her neck and shoulders.

*Mos vestiendi.*

Eleemo-
synæ.

Sir William Petty (in his book of taxes) esteems begging to be the worst way for relief of the poor. Sir Thomas Haggerston told me (this 4th day of August 1665) very much of the abuse of begging in Northumberland, and how gladly himself, Mr. Ralph Clavering and others would reform it, but they are afraid of curses and clamours. That very many Scotch beggars come into those parts, and many that are lusty and able ; yet when they have got an alms at the hall, they beg at the houses in the town, and there they get alms too for fear of their curses, although the housekeepers be less able than themselves, as being labouring men, and having no more but a cottage and a yard or garden. That the beggars wherever corn is stirring (as in winnowing, sowing, &c.) do beg, or as it were get by custom a part of the same : and to this end many go about to beg in the time of seeding. That in time of shearing he hath often faulted the reapers for unclean reaping, and that they have frequently answered, 'What shall we leave for the poor ones ?' That when he leads his corn many do come to glean in the field at the same time, so that those who should reap for hire do turn gleaners, to his great damage.

An advertisement from the Hospital called
Bedlam, printed in the Gazette about 24th June
1675, certifies that there is never any licence given
nor any plates on the arms to such wanderers as
under those colours pass up and down. When I
read this, I mentioned one Medcalf, a gentleman
who passed as a Bedlamer. Mr. Tempest and his
wife thereupon told me that he was hanged for a
murder.

On the 6th July 1673, I caused John Gorsuch   Wine
to put into the cart-house pit, about six or seven
yards north-west of the lime kiln, twelve bottles of
claret wine bottled about six weeks since (without
sugar), but not kept since that time exactly cool.
The cord in which they are threaded is put by a
noose upon the head of a stake which is driven in
a little below the surface of the water, the head
of which is about two yards from the nicks made
for a mark on the north-east of an alder tree,
which mark is about half a yard from the root of
the tree. Note, that the water is very low this
dry summer, so that it will be hard in winter to
find the cord, as the head of the stake may be
probably two or three feet under water.

T

Cattle
bought, 1664.

At Ormschurch, Whitson fair, four stirks and twinters, one for 1*l*. 9*s*. 4*d*., two for 3*l*. 3*s*. 6*d*., one for 1*l*. 14*s*. 10*d*.

,, Prescot fair, two stirks, one for 1*l*. 11*s*. 6*d*., one for 1*l*. 4*s*. 6*d*.

,, Newborough fair, five stirks or twinters, one for 1*l*. 5*s*. 6*d*., one for 1*l*. 19*s*., two for 3*l*., one for 1*l*. 9*s*. 6*d*.

Anglicè scri-
bendi modus.

It is to be marked that many things which I put down as strange expressions do within a year or two become so familiar that even I myself do wonder why I took notice of them. Which thing may put us in mind how the English language changeth in the age of a man.

Hibernicum
Bellum.

About August 1674, Richard Bellings, Esq., told me that he had almost finished the history of the Irish war for the space of about eight or nine years. He showed me a part thereof (viz. about 120 very large pages, just at the beginning of the rebellion), which I read over. I do give the greater credit to it, by reason that the said R. B. was a witness to very many things which he writes there. The said R. B. in one of his letters to me speaks of a former narrative of his own in two parts, setting forth the beginning of the commotion in Ireland.

I find the following words in the kingdom's Boscobel. 'Intelligencer,' from January 13 to January 20, 1661, p. 28 :—

'By express command from his Majesty we are to acquaint the reader that a little book named " Boscobel " (being a relation of his Majesty's happy and miraculous escape after the fight at Worcester) hath divers errors and mistakes in it, and therefore not to be admitted as a true and perfect narrative of his sacred Majesty's deliverance.'

I am not certain whether the advertisement abovesaid do relate to the first part of ' Boscobel,' or to the second, or both. For the author doth profess that he had not so good intelligence for the writing of the second as of the first. And it may be thought that this advertisement may be given to lessen the displeasure which some hot heads have conceived, that Catholics should be looked upon as the King's chief preservers next to God. But the most of the chief circumstances which we read in ' Boscobel' are confirmed by Dr. Bate's Latin history, called ' Elenchus Motuum,' &c.,

T 2

where you may read sundry more delightful things concerning the King's travels in the west of England, than Mr. Blunt (who writ ' Boscobel ') was able to relate, who wanted intelligence of the same.

Sinenses. I was at London constantly for some years last past, where, in the years 1687 and 1688, I chanced to have some conference in Latin with a natural Chinese whom I did sundry times meet with, by reason that he went to the Latin school at the Savoy. He told me that he was a native of Pekin, and that he had been about eight years absent from China. He told me that he judged Pekin to contain about double the number of the inhabitants contained in London, where he had been resident about eight months. I had formerly seen his picture admirably well painted at Windsor Castle. He appeared to be aged more than thirty years, though he pretended (and perhaps very truly) to be but five or six and twenty. He spoke to me imperfectly in Latin, as having learnt the same without any rules. I do not take him to be a competent judge of the number of people either in Pekin or in London. His stature was low and his complexion very swarthy. His nose was very flat, and his eyes, by reason that his face in that part was also flat, stood outward somewhat oddly, and were very brown ; yet his countenance was pleasing and smiling. I did likewise see in London, and had a short and free conference with Father Couplet, a Jesuit that had lived in China about twenty years. He was a native of the Spanish Netherlands, and although he was ' Sexagenario major,' he was waiting for an opportunity to pass over again to his beloved China, which was so much in his mind that, whether he was waking or sleeping, he was in a manner continually thinking of it. I did then hear him hold some short discourse in the Chinese language with that very same Chinese whom I have mentioned above, who came in unto us (when we two were only together) to ask some questions, as it seemed, of the said father.

June 3, 1676.—I saw twenty-six guineas impressed in the space of one minute, measured by my minute-watch. That coin was polished at the very same stroke (or turn) which made the impression. All this was done by one machine fed by one man and turned by three, and only one guinea

Aurum et Argentum impressum.

was impressed at each turn of the said machine or screw.   It was in the Tower of London.

Londinum.　　The present March 4, 1686–7, I took great notice at Whitehall of that famous large map (lately set out by William Morgan), of the City and Suburbs of London, where the scale of the map is such that every inch of the same represents 300 feet of the town, river, gardens, streets, &c.   The circuit is no less than eighteen or nineteen miles.   Mr. Morgan, who made the map, told me that he reckoned 1,000 paces to be a mile, which I think is eighty paces less than an English statute mile.   I do reckon the gates of London to be as follows : Ludgate, Newgate, Aldersgate, Cripplegate, Moorgate, Postern, Bishopsgate, Aldgate.

Pauli Basilica Londinensis.　　In November 1681, I took great notice of that new building, which I found then to be raised above the earth about 10 or 11 yards, according to the guess I made when I looked upon the same.   Below the surface of the earth about 14 or 16 feet the foundation seemed to be laid, and all that was hollow like a cellar.   If I be not mistaken it was arched all over, even with the top of the earth, so that there is an appearance of a church below as well as above the ground. But there was no manner of building at the west-end of the same, all being left so open that I guessed that the building would be continued much longer towards the west, which way there was then remaining, betwixt the new buildings and the ruins of the outermost part westward of the old burned church, about 80 yards or more. The east end of this new church was then close built, and the wideness there within the walls was about 41 yards, and the greatest wideness of this church was about 104 yards, whereof 11 yards on the south side and 11 yards on the north side of the same seem to be taken up in porches. At the same time I read a written paper which hung up on a wall or pillar of this new building, mentioning the contributions given towards that work by the several Bishopricks of England, the total of which amounted to 14,000*l.*, whereof London gave 2,844*l.*, Winchester 1,026*l.*, Chester 561*l.* 18*s.* 6*d.*, Durham 334*l.*, Canterbury 199*l.* I suppose there is a standing fund or revenue belonging to this same church by which in length of time it may come to be finished. There is or was, as I take it, an allowance given by Parliament out of every ton of coals coming to London.

Juramenta.    As I came down from London in June 1676, with Sergeant Rigby, who is a J.P. for Lancashire, he told me plainly once or twice upon occasion given, that the multitude of our penal laws cause them to be ill executed ; that he himself was perjured (or forsworn), for not putting the laws in execution against swearers, when he heard and saw their transgressions.    I did farther understand clearly by his expression, that he did not in the like case intend to mend his fault.

Leases.    June 27, 1663.—My nephew Selby told me that his wife's grandfather, Thomas Hesketh, Esq., did in the year 1631 and 1632 (6 and 7 Charles I.) offer to his tenants in Pilling, who had leases in being for 12 years from 7 Charles I., either to seal them new leases upon surrender of the old ones for three lives or for 33 years, i.e. for 21 years longer than their term of 12 years.    The number of leases in being were about 97, whereof 64 were renewed ; all of them but five in 7 Charles I., and those five in 8 Charles I.    Of these 64, 49 were taken for three lives and 15 for 33 years. We reckoned by the tenants' books that of these 49 leases five of them did yet retain three lives in being, 24 of them two lives in being, and 19 one life in being. So that it did appear that only one tenement of the 49 (taken about 32 years ago for three lives) had fallen to the lord. On the other hand, the 15 leases taken for 33 years are just upon the point of expiring.

This interesting record shows that the custom of granting leases for lives instead of for a term of years, which was ordinarily practised in the seventeenth century, was greatly to the disadvantage of the landlord. Yet it is doubtful if the benefit to the tenant was more than apparent. Probably, the custom was injurious both to landlord and tenant. The landlord may be said to have suffered more, for he received a very inadequate rental for his property. It was Mr. Blundell's practice to give an old tenant a lease for three lives at the rate of seven years' purchase. Thus, if a farm was worth annually 10*l.*, he got 70*l.* for the lease with some other trifling allowances, and lost all control over his property for the next thirty, forty, or fifty years, if any of the three lives lasted so long. There was something paid annually by way of ground rent, but the amount was very small. The tenant, on the other hand, having had difficulty in raising the capital required to enter upon the farm, had seldom anything to expend upon his place, which fell into dilapidation often long before the tenancy expired. He had no stimulus to industry, and generally contented himself with an easy and careless management, provided he secured a moderate maintenance for himself. Moreover, he or some of those belonging to him might, and often did, render themselves particularly obnoxious to their landlord, whose hands were tied by the lease. 'Moore's Rental,' published by the Cheetham Society, and written by Sir Edward Moore, first Baronet of Bank Hall, Mr. Blundell's contemporary and neighbour, contains very severe strictures upon the conduct of his tenants. It is true that these were mostly leaseholders residing in the adjacent town (Liverpool), whose interests as townsmen would often clash with those of their landlord. Still, the same spirit manifested itself in country places. Mr. Nicholas Blundell, grandson to the Cavalier, frequently complains of the behaviour of certain tenants, and recommends his successor to discard them when their leases expire. The custom of leasing for lives was discontinued upon the Crosby Estate about a century ago, and although it lingered in the neighbourhood for another half-century, it is now almost universally abandoned.

Pilling in the Fylde lies on the borders of Morecambe Bay, and its once extensive moss (reduced gradually by cultivation) is still frequented by large flocks of sea-birds which build there annually. Pilling was a possession of Cockersand Abbey, purchased at the dissolution by John Kitchin, whose daughter conveyed a portion of it to the Daltons, on whose estate of Thurnham lie the ruins of the abbey. These ruins are not extensive, but the chapter-house has been covered in, and is used as a family Mausoleum by the Daltons. The abbey

stood at the edge of the sands, through the midst of
which the small river Cocker flows towards the sea.
Hence its ancient name, but in these days it is commonly called Thurnham Abbey. The Hall is in the
immediate neighbourhood, and is an old rambling
manor-house, built at different periods and not without that usual adjunct to ancient Catholic dwellings,
a priest's hiding-place. There is more than one
place of this kind, and the writer remembers to have
noticed that they differ from others that he has seen,
in respect that they are entered by the removal of a
square stone in the wall. This plan of construction
was adopted in order that no hollow sound might
betray their purpose. The Dalton family is now represented by Sir Gerald Dalton Fitzgerald, Bart.

Barnaby Kitchin, who died July 6, 1603, held
the other moiety of Pilling, and married—

> 1st. Ann, daughter of Sir John Aughton, of
> North Meols, Esq., by whom he had one
> daughter—
>> Alice, born 1554 = Hugh Hesketh, natural
>> son of Sir Thomas Hesketh of Rufford,
>> Knight.
> 2nd. Alice, widow of William Forshaw, Esq., by
> whom he had two daughters—
>> Anne, born 1582 = Thomas Ashton.
>> Elizabeth, born 1587 = Nathaniel, son and
>> heir of Nicholas Banastre, of Altham, Esq.

In 1649, a partition of Barnaby Kitchin's Pilling
estate was made, when Pilling Hall and one-third
of the demesne fell to Richard, son of Nathaniel
Banastre, one-third to Richard, son of Thomas
Ashton, and the remaining third to Thomas and
Robert, sons of Hugh Hesketh. This Thomas was

grandfather to Mrs. Selby, who had likewise inherited
North Meols from the Aughtons.   This latter township is that on which the modern town of Southport
is built.   At the death of Mrs. Selby, without issue,
her estate reverted to her uncle, Robert Hesketh,
whose descendant still possesses one moiety of North
Meols.   The Hornbys, of Poulton, purchased the
Banastre and Ashton shares of Pilling in 1678, and
the remaining third in 1772.   They are now held by
E. G. S. Hornby, Esq., of Dalton Hall.   (Fishwick's
Garstang, vol. ii. Chetham Society.)

*Justitia ci-*
*vilis.*

I was told on October 24, 1683, by Mr. Thomas
Bootle, that whereas two shillings is always paid in
our neighbourhood to the Justice's Clerk for a
warrant even in case of felony and of like crimes
against the King, that at Manchester there is paid
no more than one shilling and sixpence for such
warrants.   William Norres, who was clerk to Justice Blundell in King James' time, told me oft,
that in those days the clerks took not one penny
for any such warrant.

*Gallicum*
*idioma.*

I did first of all in this my 58th year begin to
study French, with design to understand it in a
book, and I find it is not hard to do so.   It is too
late for me to begin with things of this nature,
but I have an honest design, though no great hope
to effect it.

There should be a north-west passage found, or rather a north-east passage, for the attaining of the Latin tongue. The inseparable difficulties of Latin do arise chiefly from hence, that we pretend to the understanding of Latin which hath been writ in all places and ages for about 2,000 years, whereas we are not able to understand our English Chaucer who lived but 300 years ago. And the several dialects of our own little country used at this day are not understood by any one person. The vulgar tongues are more easy. In September 1677, I knew not so much of French as to understand the meaning of *moi, toi, elle,* or the like most usual words, yet in March next following (having spent in reading French, an hour or two in the interim each day for the most part, and still without the help of a dictionary) I began to read the first part of the abridgment of the 'Holy History.' It was composed by Du Verdier, and consists of 574 pages octavo. I read this book twice over in French with much delight, as understanding the story sufficiently well without the help of an English translation. This I did in the space of twenty-six days, spending little time but only after supper, and yet during these twenty-six days I had five fits of an ague. My memory was then very bad, as being dulled with age and cares, yet my knowledge of Latin and English I think did advance me more, by three parts in four, than if I had only understood some one other language or two which had affinity with the French. I judge that I myself and others of my small bore have in our younger days spent fifteen-fold more labour and time in the study of Latin only, without attaining that degree of knowledge therein which I got as above in French. So that it is not to be doubted, though Latin be very hard, but that it is a ready means to the knowledge of the best modern languages of Europe. I must not conceal that I was helped in reading the French book abovesaid by the knowledge which I had of the story, and although I wanted a dictionary, I had a good French grammar from which I learned much.

*Apparatus de Catholicis Anglicanis.*

Many things have been said well by way of apology for Catholics, and more may be said hereafter as occasion shall serve. In the year 1661, I printed a small book on that subject which I have showed to few, and I think it was never exposed to sale. It is entitled '*Quid me persequeris?*'

There are remarkable things in it which may do well now (1678) when the state of things is changed, being put into a better method.

> No printed copy of this work has been found, but it is the title Mr. Blundell gave to his treatise on the Penal Laws, referred to in the introductory chapters.

Cherlotta, daughter of the Duke of Trimouil, is now the widow of James Earl of Derby, who was beheaded for his fidelity to the King, 1651, October 15. She was pleased to tell me (December 14, 1659) that she was then one of the five heirs to Madam Mamsel d'Orange, whose estate was 60,000*l.* per annum. There was then a report that that lady was to marry King Charles, which Lady Derby seemed heartily to wish, though it was like to destroy her own expectation. The Duke, her brother, refused (as she said) 100 years' purchase from Richelieu for his Dukedom, but answered that he would part with that and his life together. It may be I did mistake some of these stories by defect of my Lady's English.

*Derbiæ Comitessa.*

It is reported that Sir Kenelm Digby ( a person very famous for valour and other great parts)

*Duellum &c.*

did receive a challenge from a certain young cour-
tier, whose reputation in that kind was yet in
question, and his person (by lowness of stature) a
little contemptible. But this challenge was flatly
refused by Sir K., and when the young spark com-
plained that he had blemished his honour, and
therefore did not deal like a gentleman to deny
him a way to clear it, Sir K. replied that he would
give it him under his hand, that Sir Kenelm Digby
had refused to fight a duel with Mr. A. B. So
confidently may a known and valiant spirit slight
all the rash contempts of an inferior person. But
when the same Sir Kenelm was provoked in the
King's presence (upon occasion of the old business
of Scanderoon) by the Venetian Embassador, who
told the King it was very strange that his Majesty
should slight so much his ancient amity with the
most noble state of Europe, for the affection which
he bare to a man (meaning Sir K.) whose father
was a traitor, his wife a wh——e, and himself a pirate,
altho he made not the least reply (as long as the
Embassador remained in England) to those great
reproaches, yet after, when the quality of his enemy
was changed (by his return) to that of a private
person, Sir Kenelm posted after him into Italy.

There sending him a challenge to Venice (from some neighbouring state), he found the discreet Magnifico as silent in Italy as himself had been before in England, and so he returned home.

But how shall a gentleman refuse a challenge without a note of cowardice, whose valour hath not yet been testified ? This let the following story teach you :—

Mr. Langley of Shropshire sent a challenge to Mr. Owen, a gentleman of the same county, to provoke him, on pretence of an injury, to a single duel. Owen returns a denial, alleging the laws of God and of the nation for so doing, and addeth further that he shall never decline his usual and well-known walks for any fear of Langley, who may find him when he pleaseth with his sword by his side, which he shall not doubt but to manage in his own defence, to the damage of a future assailant. Langley hereupon assails him in his walk, but is opposed strongly and in fine disarmed. He sends him after this a second challenge, but receiving the same answer, he assaulteth his adversary again in the former manner and just with the former success. After all this ado, nothing would serve our unfortunate champion but a third adventure, which proving just the same in all kinds of respects with the other two, finding himself condemned, and the other as much extolled by all the country, he was content at length to be quiet. *Narravit mihi* Ds. Geo. Fox, January 22, 1659. Mr. Langley lives now in Shrewsbury.

George Lord Digby (now Earl of Bristol) about the year 1649, when he went out of Ireland into France, was met at his landing by the Lord Wilmot, who provoked his Lordship to a single duel upon an old difference in England betwixt the Lord Digby, as Chief of the faction at Court, and the soldiers of fortune patronised by Prince Rupert, and mainly strengthened by the Lords Gerard and Wilmot. This challenge was refused by the Lord Digby with much civility and fair words, commiserating the loss of so much English·loyal blood as had been spilt in the late war, and lamenting withal the fewness of his Majesty's surviving servants. The Lord Wilmot, interpreting all this mildness to proceed from weakness of courage, did reproach him unworthily with it, but could not for all that wrest his Lordship a jot from his fixed resolution. At the last he told him the Prince Rupert, esteeming him unworthy to die by his sword, had vowed to shoot him dead at their first meeting. But here the Lord Digby changeth his copy, and that which he would not before accept in defence of his own honour, he offers now to his enemy in defence of another. For charging the Lord Wilmot grievously for having aspersed so basely a person of so great worth and a Prince of the Royal blood of England, he requireth satisfaction with his sword for the Prince's honour. So by the help of his wit changing the state of the quarrel, he is now become Prince Rupert's champion, and to approve himself right worthy of that honour he worsteth the Lord Wilmot in the duel, and is afterwards reconciled to his other great enemies who had intended to have fought him upon the same old quarrel.

> This encounter between Lords Digby and Wilmot occurred in 1647, as we learn by a letter from Robert Thorner to Sir R. Verney, dated Paris, in October of that year. 'Lord Digby, O'Neal, and Mr. Digby, son to Sir Kenelm, on Thursday last disarmed the Lord Wilmot, the Lord Wentworth, and his second, to their great dishonour.' (See Collections of Sir William Verney, Bart., in 'Historical Commissioners' Appendix to 7th Report.')

It is said that there is a certain eel in the sea which is called the whale thrasher, as big as a

*Cete ab anguillis vapulantur.*

X 2

small mast of a ship, and that there is a confederacy betwixt this eel and the sword fish to
destroy the whales. Whereupon the sword fish
going under the whale's belly, pricketh the tender
parts thereof in such sort as that the whale to
avoid the hurt raiseth himself above the water.
Then comes the sliding eel upon his back, and
having seized fast about his head, she raiseth her
tail aloft like a whip and belaboureth his sides and
back with continual lashes, until with the assistance
of her undermining companion they have effected
their design by the death of their unwieldy enemy.
Captain Hill (once a pirate at sea, afterwards a lay-
brother with the Jesuits) told Mr. Waldgrave (from
whom I had the relation, February 8, 1659) that
once as he sailed, he saw such an eel for the space
of half-an-hour thrashing the sides of a whale in
such manner as is aforesaid.

This looks like an early appearance of the sea-
serpent.

Ver tardans
aliquando
festinans.
I have observed that in such springs as are
neither forward nor backward, our apple trees are
fully yet freshly blossomed on May-day, yet have
I noted in a very backward year, that very few

apple-tree buds have on that day put forth any manner of reddish colour and cast no flower at all. I have noted in my almanac about the year 1669 (as I take it), that on the 3rd of May I could not discern, as I passed closely by the side of the orchard at Haigh, so much as the least red or white upon any apple bud.

A.D. 1679–80, January 30, white violets were plucked in my garden, and daffodils in great number budded and near breaking out, as to the flower. Plenty of tansy about a finger long. On the 1st February many of our apricock buds were red. Some hawthorn leaves were in February as broad as a silver twopence, many were so. On 30th March 1680, very many of my summer russetting apple blossoms were full blown. Our pear trees fully flowered, and in their greatest lustre, March 25, 1680.

Very many barren wives do so strongly fancy themselves to be with child, that they do even send for the midwife as being ready to bring forth, when yet there is no conception. One of my acquaintance fancied herself to be pregnant ten years together. The fanatical wife of a baronet, at such

*Observationes politicæ.*

time as her preacher came to give her a visit, said, 'As soon as the voice of your salutation sounded in my ears, the babe leaped in my womb.' Yet was she never with child.

1666, September 26.—Winefrid Blundell, writing to a lady of rank who had applied to her for a servant, says, ' I have engaged her for 15*s.* for a quarter, which is all the time agreed for. I have heard that our country-women are generally esteemed much better servants than I can for the present furnish your Ladyship with, but both the best and indifferent sort are of a humour which must be dealt with (now and then) by giving some little sweet encouragement, and not always by severity. They will commonly for a great fault endure a severe check, but not for every small one, and sometimes they must know it if they do well, &c.'

Mr. Blundell's sister Winefrid, in giving the above advice to her correspondent, evinced a thorough knowledge of the 'humour' of servant-girls from that part of Lancashire, which remains unchanged to this day ; the last touch is admirable.

It is well known that this day, 1650, Cromwell won the famous battle of Dunbar, and on the same day, 1651, the great battle of Worcester. On that day, 1658, he ended his own life. The same day, 1662, William Lenthall, Speaker of the Long Parliament, did likewise die. I have heard that Wednesday, as I take it, hath been fatal to the house of Derby. I was born, contracted to my wife, and lamed with a shot upon Saturday, on which day my father died.

The greatest gamblers are those who in public *Aleæ lusus.* gaming houses, called the offices of insurance, do for a sum of money secure buildings upon the land from fire, and ships upon the sea from water, &c.

> If the writer had lived in these times and seen the accounts of the great insurance companies, he would have retracted this sweeping condemnation. In his day, the few risks of this nature that were taken up were incurred by single individuals, and this certainly wears the appearance of reckless gambling.

Our manner of writing in this age is too exact *Anglicè scribendi modus.* and wholly turned into points (and witticisms), the continuation of which is impossible. Mr. Gui Miege set forth his great French and English Dictionary, price 30*s.*, about the year 1688. There is in it his English Grammar, which I take to be much better than any I have seen. The word 'cozen' is writ twenty-nine different ways.

The book called 'Britannia Languens,' p. 131 (note that the pages there for a long way together are false printed), speaking of the poor of England, says that they are increased by computation to near ten times the late number, within the last twenty years, and that their maintenance doth cost the nation 400,000*l.* per annum constant tax.

In July 1684, I asked a poor woman how many children she had. She answered, 'Six.' 'Here,' said I, 'here is sixpence for them.' 'No, sir,' said she, most simply, 'I will not sell my children.'

| | Baptisms | Burials | | Baptisms | Burials |
|---|---|---|---|---|---|
| 1663 | 158 | 212 | 1671 | 163 | 182 |
| 1664 | 254 | 172 | 1672 | 209 | 307 |
| 1665 | 174 | 282 | 1673 | 191 | 213 |
| 1666 | 205 | 176 | 1674 | 166 | 288 |
| 1667 | 174 | 212 | 1675 | 164 | 231 |
| 1668 | 192 | 242 | 1676 | 174 | 242 |
| 1669 | 187 | 230 | 1677 | 206 | 224 |
| 1670 | 194 | 143 | 1678 | — | 210 |

A bashful man is not his own master, nor uses his own judgment, but is overawed by the boldness of others, and they that are impudent have a power over him. Bashfulness is sometimes a friend, but more often an evil guardian to youth, betraying it, contrary to its own desire and inclination, to the worst of men, who hurry it to evil actions and places. How many men have lost their estates, honour, and lives, because they were ashamed to distrust. A man invites you to game, drink, rob, or to be bound for him. This foolish modesty is to be cast off. Deny him. An impudent flatterer comes to eat upon you ; he begs a horse, a ring, or garment of you. Give to the deserver ; respect not him that begs. Some are so bashful as not to send for a good physician, nor employ a good lawyer, because they are acquainted with a worse. Begin betimes to break this fault, and in small matters to assert your own liberty ; deny to debauch, deny to lend money, or to admire everyone you hear praised ; be constant, and be not overcome by importunity which is a part of impudence, needful (perhaps) to them that know not otherwise how to live.

Some men ask pardon where there is no offence, but when it is commanded by God and reason, they will rather die than do it. *Officiosa verba.*

Y

*Procellæ.*

In August 1662, there happened a hail-storm in these west parts of Lancashire, whereby many fields of good corn were quite destroyed in an instant. Some parts of Sefton parish (especially the Lunt), some parts of Halsall, Aughton, and Ormskirk parishes, did suffer very much damage. Pigeons were killed thereby, fruit spoiled, and the boughs of trees cloven and slit with the hail-stones.

In February 1661, there was a short storm of wind, which exceeded (as some affirm) all that have been known in these parts. Sundry buildings and some orchards in Cheshire were quite overturned. And the damage to ships in Liverpool was such, as the like (in no proportion) could ever be remembered.

*Ruperti Principis maritima expeditio.*

Mr. Humphrey Bagarley lent me a MS. of this expedition, writ by an eye-witness, wherein I find this. That Prince Rupert and his brother Prince Maurice began this voyage from Helvoet-sluys A.D. 1648, in January. He returned to Nantes in March 1652–3. He had many sad disasters, but made no considerable fight in the whole voyage, which was most of it spent in and about the West Indies. Prince Maurice was lost in the night, driven upon a rock (as was supposed) by Ireland. Prince Rupert's ship, towards the end of the year 1652, was sunk by a leak, wherein perished 333 persons, who forced him to save his life by the help of a small pleasure boat. The story of that is very long and tragical. Prince Rupert was wounded with an arrow in Affrick. They took some prizes, but not many. This relation is not well penned, nor is it at all exact in the chief particulars.

Her letter to my sister Frances, dated March 23 (it came into my hands, May 1674), tells that she was at the writing of it in as great a depth of misery and grief of heart as ever she was since her dear husband and children left her. That her house and lands were fallen into my lord's hands for want of payment of rent. That she cannot get money to pay the rent, but is at suit for 10*l.*, which is owing to her, but that the officers cannot give her justice till an officer come from the old Bishop who banished her. That the officers have given her a letter to him (who is at London), but that she knows not well how to get it thither. That she is tabled with her daughter Ratclif at a

Cannel the widow.

market town, fifteen miles from her own house, but
her son Ratclif having come to some loss by her,
she finds a change in some things. That her
daughter Cannel's husband aims to get her lands,
who asked in the face of the Court why they suffered her to live there ? and who would live in a
house with a papist ? They were bloody, and he
would not live with any of them. He swore the
peace against her, and that he was afraid she would
burn his house upon him, and so she was ordered
to put in sureties or go to prison. That her health
is worse and worse each day, and that her grief is
great for want of the Sacraments. She intends to
come over to her daughter Jane (if Jane's husband
be content) for one year.

> This unfortunate gentlewoman was a daughter
> of Thomas Hesketh of Meols, Esq., and had mar-
> ried Deemster Cannel of the Isle of Man, from
> whence she writes this pitiful letter. She was re-
> lated to Mr. Blundell through the Norris's of Speke,
> her grandmother, wife of Mr. Molineux of the
> Wood, being sister to Edward Norris, Esq. We find
> from his book of accounts that Mr. Blundell fre-
> quently extended his charity to her and her im-
> poverished family. She seems to have had a
> daughter settled at Crosby, and no fewer than five
> of her children became Religious abroad.

October 1, 1677.—My son made a large firkin, two parts and more of orange apples, the rest were large sour apples. The liquor was strained through a cloth and stood two days in a large vessel, then was it drawn into a firkin and stopped up.

October 5th and 6th.—I made three firkins of cider—one of orange apples, one of Harrison's apples, and one of grove apples. All these were turned immediately into the firkins. The two first were stopped up the second day, the last stopped up the first day. Some small vent was left in all. The second had far more pills and uncleanness in it than the rest. I put some wheat into the first and second when I made them up. We had generally near a third part of liquor proportionable to the measure of the apples. The grove apples, which made the last firkin, were got about eighteen hours before they were pressed. The rest were plucked or shaken some days before. The five firkins contained, I think, one hogshead.

A list of the names of Popish Recusants of the greatest quality in the county of Lanc^e to be

*[Marginal note: Cider.]*

*[Marginal note: Banishment of Recusants.]*

banished by Act of Parliament, held October
1680 :—

> Caryll Lord Viscount Molyneux.
> Wm. Molyneux, Esq.
> Sir William Gerard, Bart.
> Sir Chas. Anderton, Bart.
> Wm. Molyneux of Croxteth, Esq.
> Richd. Sherburne of Stonyhurst, Esq.
> Ricd. Walmesley of Dunkenhalgh, Esq.
> Edmd. Trafford of Trafford, Esq.
> Edmd. Tildesley of the Lodge, Esq.
> Thos. Tildesley his son.
> Ralph Tildesley.
> Humphrey Trafford.
> Robt. Dalton of Thurnham, Esq.
> Hugh Dicconson of Wrightington, Esq.
> Hy. Blundell of Ince Blundell, Esq.
> John Harrington of Huyton, Esq.
> Wm. Blundell of Crosby, Esq.
> Richd. Butler of Rawcliffe, Esq.
> Wm. Hesketh of Singleton, Esq.
> Thos. Stanley of Eccleston, Esq.
> John Brockholes of Claughton, Esq.
> Robt. Molyneux of the Wood, Esq.
> Sir Rowland Bellasis, Bart.
> Richd. Towneley of Towneley, Esq.
> S. Langton of Abraham, Esq.
> — Eccleston of Eccleston, Esq.
> — Scarisbrick of Scarisbrick, Esq.
> Thos. Culcheth of Culcheth, Esq.
> Thos. Braithwaite of L'pool, Esq.
> Richd. Chorley of Chorley, Esq.
> Richd. Grimshaw of Clayton, Esq.

Richd. Sherburne of Stonyhurst, gent.
Wm. Standish of Wigan, gent.
Wm. Blundell, Jr. of Crosby, gent.
Wm. Dicconson of Wrightington, gent.
Alexr. Standish of Standish, gent.
Richd. Gerard of Ince, gent.
Chrisr. Anderton of Wigan, gent.
George Carus of Whittington, gent.
Thos. Lydiate of Lydiate, gent.
Wm. Wolfall of Huyton and Roby, gent.
Edmd. Stanley of Aughton, gent.
Thos. Stanley of Aughton, gent.
Thos. Worthington, Senr. of Wigan, gent.
Chas. Harris of Bowland, gent.
Cuthbt. Hesketh of Goosenargh, gent.
Edmd. Threlfall of Goosenargh, gent.
Thos. Gooden of Pendlebury, gent.
Edmd. Gooden of Little Bolton, gent.
Jas. Duckett of Ashton, gent.
Christr. Hayes of Bulk, gent.
Richd. Massy of Ashton (q. Rixton), gent.
George Leybourne of Nateby, gent.
Hy. Gerard of Bamfurlong, gent.
Wm. Anderton of Euxton, gent.
Edmd. Standish of Worthington, gent.
Peregrine Tasburgh of Ormskirk, gent.
Geo. Westby of Up. Rawcliffe, gent.
Josh. Bryer of Lathom, gent.
Bernard Westby of Manor, gent.
Wm. Money of Dunkenhalgh, gent.
Geo. Culcheth of Towneley, gent.
Thos. Knype of Dalton, gent.
Wm. Fazakerley of Liverpool, gent.

This list was sent by Mr. John Gelibrond to Mr. Blundell, and he says that it is imperfect in names and places, but is a true copy of the list given by Lord Ancram to Sir Roger Bradshaigh.

1624, October 19.—A speeche of a bargain with Nichs. Hewett Brikeman for the making of eight schore thousand breekes :—

The claye must be feighed, upon my master's charges and a horse and carte fownde during the tyme of moulding ; a moulding boarde and three whyte barrows ; a bearing barrow and a burbette to keep water.

He must have 2s. 9d. for a thowsand breeke. The breeke must be 10 in. long, 5 in. broade, and $2\frac{1}{2}$ in. thicke, which cometh to the sum of 22l. The payment of that he would have at three tymes viz., at the carting (which must be as soon as my master can make ready for it) the sum of 5l. 10s. ; at the moulding, 11l., and at the burning 5l. 10s. Towards the burning there must be provided twenty tunne of coale and sixty tunne of slacke, ten loade of woode and three of turfe. He must have two beds found him, and housing fitting to lay his bed and dressing meat, and a cow grass during the tyme of moulding, which will be about Whitsuntide ; the tyme of burning must be abowte St. James' tide (July 25)

> Although this memorandum is before the time of the Cavalier, it is inserted on account of its interest, as regards the price of building material early in the seventeenth century. It points also to the period when large additions were made to Crosby Hall, and when probably the older portions of the house were demolished.

I fee'd an attorney (Mr. Samuel Andrews) after my conviction at the Assizes, and thus he writ to me August 26, 1673 :—' I have enquired in the Crown Office at Lancaster, and am informed by the clerks there that you are not in any danger of conviction till the next assizes at soonest. The course being, that such presentments as were brought in at the last assizes are at the next drawn up into a formal bill and found by Grand Inquest, and at the latter end of that assize (if prosecution be intended against them) their names are read up and a proclamation made, that unless they conform before the then next assizes, or in the mean time render their bodies to the Sheriff (this seems grounded upon two several statutes, viz., 29 Eliz. cap. vi. and 3 James, cap. iv) they will be convict. So that I conceive (supposing a vigorous prosecution be intended, which I hope is not), there can be no conviction against you until next summer assizes, unless the Justices of the Peace at their Quarter Sessions proceed against you, which the statute of 3 James, cap. iv. directs.

Cruces, &c.  The Lord Scudamore caused a marble altar table to be taken from Abbey Dore in Herefordshire, and brought to his own house, Holme. In the carriage whereof one of his servants had his leg broken and another was killed outright. The table or stone was used in his house for the pressing of cheeses. But the cheeses that were pressed therewith did run blood, whereupon it was removed to the laundry for the linens to be washed and batted upon it. Then again it was observed that a continual noise of batting upon the said stone was heard in the night, whereupon the stone was taken by the command of the said lord to the place from whence he had taken it. This happened about seven or eight or ten years ago and was told to me by Mr. Stanton, November 7, 1660. He heard the relation from one Mr. Scudamore, a priest, for whom the Lord Scudamore had sent to advise with him concerning the fore-mentioned prodigies. Mr. Stanton did likewise hear the son of the said lord, when he told the same story to other persons.

There was a stone cross standing at Whalley on the side of a bowling green which was found one day when the bowlers were come to play to be thrown down upon the green ; and in regard it lay in their way, they desired to have it removed off the green. Whereupon an able strong man that was present reared up the stele or shaft of the said cross upon one end ; and because it was too heavy to be otherwise removed by a single person, he wrested it from edge to edge (keeping the higher end all the while in his arms), intending in that manner to have removed it off the green. But it pleased God that while the man was labouring hard to effect his purpose, he fell down flat upon his back, and the stone falling upon his breast killed him outright, so that he uttered never a word. The news of this strange accident coming to a house in the neighbourhood, a certain man who heard the relation cried out immediately, that some sudden death would undoubtedly betide himself, because (said he), that same man and my-

self did, this very last night, privately pull down
the cross that hath now killed him.

This relation I had from William Norris of
Blackrod, gentleman, January 3, 1660, who told
me that he had it from Mr. Richard Craven of
Dinkley, about thirty years since ; who told him
that he himself was an eye-witness when the man
was killed.

Whittaker in his 'History of Whalley' makes
no mention of the latter remarkable circumstance.

*Tituli vanis
simi.*

When the King of Morocco expressed his
wonder to the Embassador sent from King Charles
of England, that so mighty a prince as his master
was entitled so poorly ; the Embassador returned
answer that many of his titles were left out for
brevity sake, for besides the dominion of Great
Britain, his master was likewise King of Northumberland, Cumberland, and Westmoreland, and of
many other places no less considerable ; which
answer did abundantly satisfy.

*Observa-
tiones piæ.*

In the use of excessive gaming my passions
have been very great and many—viz. hope, fear,
joy, sadness, &c., but above all anger.   And I do
believe that my passions have been more frequent

and violent about this one thing, than upon any one other occasion, hitherto, in the course of my life. Yet see the folly of this. The sense of those things at gaming which troubled or rejoiced me so much, was commonly so inconstant and short, that within one hour or two (especially at tables, and at all other games of dice), I had quite forgot the occasions of my several passions. And now at this present all those things which have formerly troubled me so much do seem no more to concern me than if they had been only dreams. I am therefore persuaded that if I had now the courage to leave the superfluous things of this world (which trouble and solicit me so much), I should within a short time be no more concerned in the want of them than I am now concerned in those desires and passions which I have had long since at play and which are now all forgotten.

The many great virtues and high abilities in sundry kinds of my dear brother Richard have been told unto me by divers persons who have lived long in his company, some of whom were present at his death. These were Mr. Thomas Bradshaigh, Mr. Kempe, Mr. Christopher Brad-

*Richard Blundell.*

shaigh, Mr. Edwards, Mr. Walgrave, Mr. Cotton,
and sundry others. His learning and judgment
were so great that the Italians would point him
out in the streets with these words, 'There goeth
the great English Wit.' He lived at Rome but
about three years at the most, yet he had learnt
the Italian language ; he spake Greek so perfectly
that he frequently repaired to the natural Greeks
in Rome to hold discourse in their own language.
He wrote a pretty book in Latin (which is now in
my hands), concerning the nature of meteors, and
another small book in English, wherein he did
epitomise the chief part of Sir Kenelm Digby's
book of Bodies. His nature was lively and cheerful, and exceeding sociable and grateful. He was
very exemplary in his life and conversation, inso-
much that I have been credibly informed that the
remarkable passages of his life are collected and
read frequently in the college where he lived and
died, for the example of others. One of the
above-named persons, who was his dear friend and
chamber-fellow in the college, did inform me that
he hath sundry times invited him, especially upon
the eves of some notable feasts, to retire into their
chambers, where they have offered to God certain

devotions and sharp disciplines for the good of their native country. Sundry of the persons above mentioned appeared so extremely affected to his memory, that I have heard them make long and feeling discourses of many of these particulars, and of other notable things concerning his life and death.

Mr. Henry Long, who came this year, 1666, from Rome, told me that to this day there is a great memory even among the Italians at Rome of my brother Richard, and that he hath heard sundry of them much extol his great abilities. He told me with what great applause my said brother did make his public defension of Philosophy in the Roman College, and that the famous divine and philosopher, Father Geteen, did dispute against him. This Mr. Long told me, December 16, 1666.

Richard Blundell, born 1625-6, entered the English College, Rome, September 7, 1645. At that time he made the following answers to the usual interrogatories :—' My name is Richard, youngest son of Nicholas Blundell and Jane Bradshaw, who on account of divers persecutions for the orthodox faith fled from her native country of Lancashire into Cheshire, and there brought me into the world her eleventh child ; but ten days after my birth sent me back to her own home to be nursed, and there I lived to my thirteenth year under various tutors, both Catholic and Protestant, but with little fruit.

My present condition is not unlike that of my country, that is, miserable. Only in this I consider myself happy, that, snatched away from all the troubles of my friends, I am so fortunately landed at this port of happiness. But notwithstanding that my parents were oppressed by the multitude of their children, they have provided for each one an annual pension for their respectable maintenance. My father, son of William Blundell, Esq., was born, or at least suckled, in prison, where his parents lay for a long time on account of their faith. He, when a youth, married Jane, the eldest daughter of Roger Bradshaw, Esq., the fruit of which marriage was thirteen children, of whom six only are now alive who, left orphans, mourn over the premature deaths of their parents. All my relations to a man, as far as I know, are and always were Catholics. Of these four uncles are priests, two sisters and three (paternal) aunts, nuns. Besides these I have many other connections. When I was thirteen years old, I went to St. Omer's College,' &c. He died at the English College, of fever, on August 7, 1649. On his deathbed he was received into the Society of Jesus, having long had the desire of entering it. In fact, his fever was occasioned, as his intimate friend and schoolfellow Father Waldegrave declared, by his great travel through the streets of Rome during the heat of summer to obtain by the interest of certain cardinals a dispensation from his college oath. An interesting memoir of this pious youth, containing many edifying particulars, will be found in Brother Foley's ' Records S. J.' vol. i. It was written by

Father George Gray, and is addressed to Father Richard Bradshaigh, his uncle. A copy of this document is amongst the 'Crosby Papers.'

It must be remembered that the term English 'Wit,' as applied to R. Blundell, would then have a much wider signification than it has at the present day.

On Thursday, August 11, 1664, the Earls of Castlehaven and Arran (whereof the first was about fifty years of age or very near it), in St James' Park, upon a wager laid with the King, killed a fat strong buck by running on foot, having each a knife in his hand. They had six hours to perform it, but they did it in two and a half. They were a good while before they could unherd him. Then they run him till, being extremely hot, he took the water in a pond where they threw stones at him, and toiled, and drove him so to a side, till they killed him with their knives. This was told me by a gentleman that was present when the buck was killed, and the thing is very true.

*Dama cursu duorum virorum superatus.*

James Touchet, second son of Mervyn Touchet, Baron Audley and Earl of Castlehaven, executed on Tower Hill for infamous crimes, had a new patent of his father's titles in 1634. Was general of the Irish army which acted against Cromwell and the Parliament. After the subjugation of Ireland, he retired to France, but returned to England when the King came back. Was restored in 1678 to all the honours forfeited by his father, and died October 11, 1684. His brother succeeded to his titles, but the Earldom expired in 1777. The Barony of Audley, being a barony in fee, has descended through the last Earl's sister to the present Lord Audley.

Lord Richard Butler, second son of James, first Duke of Ormond, was created Earl of Arran in 1662. Became a Peer of England under the title of Baron Butler of Weston, 1673. He distinguished himself in the naval engagement of that year, and later on, in 1682, he did good service in Ireland. He died in 1685 without male issue, though he had been twice married.

Jesu
Societas.

The Fathers do accustom themselves to public disciplines in their colleges on the eves of great feasts. *Narravit mihi unus ex illis.* The same party told me that when the Swede was expected in Lithuania, the Fathers in Vilna, whereof he was one, did take a bloody discipline each day for a whole month to avert the displeasure of God.

I told Father Richard Banister (who had been Provincial the year before), that one great cause of the disaffection of some Englishmen to the Jesuits in England was the false apprehension of the greatness of their number in this province. To which he answered that he knew for certain that there were not in England at that time 150 Jesuits, and said, if an account were taken, he would be content to die, &c., if the number were so many. 1661.

Sir Edward Widdrington showed me a picture of a Frenchman who, he said, had killed twenty-two men in single duel, and was finally slain himself in such a combat. Duellum.

Baron Limbeck, a Burgundian (yet living, 1660) had eight brothers slain in duels. He fought a famous combat, as one of the six subjects of Spain, against the like number of French who were under the Prince of Condé. They fought upon post horses to prevent inequality of management. Two of the French were slain, and the Spaniards got the day. *Narravit mihi* Mr. Jo. Molineux, February 16, 1660.

Baron Botavil was a most desperate, implacable duellist. He was beheaded for this in Place Royale, having killed divers men even upon mere shadows of affronts.—*Idem narravit.*

Lewis XI., King of France, had granted a pardon four or five times to one who had killed so many men in duels. He asked his Confessor whether he might lawfully pardon him any more, the like occasion being then happened. The Confessor replied that the King might do it as well then as he had done it the first time. For the murderer had only killed one single man, the King (who had pardoned that) killed all the rest.

*Hispaniola.*    The story is very famous of the fleet which was sent by Cromwell to subdue this island about the year 1655, where as they marched through the woods to surprise St. Domingo, a great part of the army was routed and destroyed by one troop of about fifty horsemen. After which repulse the remainder of the army went and took Jamaica. In the year 1673, I was told by owner William Williamson of Liverpool that he was at Hispaniola at the same time, and upon Easter day he saw the English army mustered there, and that the muster-master, being his friend, told him that the army mustered was 9,774, of which number 1,200 were seamen and no more.

*Fœtifera familia.*    In or about the year 1673 there happened in one family in Salford, within the space of twenty-four hours, these several births following, viz.: the wife of the house was delivered of a son, a cow of a calf, a sow of fifteen pigs, a bitch of sixteen whelps, a cat of four kittens, and a hen hatched fourteen eggs. All this I took in writing from Mr. Samuel Andrews, and he professed that he had it credibly affirmed to him by persons in the same neighbourhood.

September 2, 1666, a fire began in London, Londinum. and in four or five days burned the greater part of the city. Mr. Thomas Massey in his letter to me from thence, October 9, 1666, saith that of 410 acres within the city, the which hath been measured, there are 335 burnt and 64 out of the city.

'The London Gazette,' ending April 30, 1666, tells us of Colonel John Rathbone and seven more old rebels, found guilty at the Old Bailey for plotting the King's death and surprisal of the Tower, &c. The 2nd and 3rd September was pitched on for the attempt, as being found by 'Lilly's Almanack,' and a scheme erected for the purpose, to be a lucky day, and a planet then ruling which prognosticated the downfall of the monarchy.

I saw a great brass gun mounted over the cliff Tormenta cærulia. at Dover Castle, A.D. 1660. It was (I take it)

both in repute and appearance about 24 feet long,
made in Utrecht about 200 years before. It
seemed to carry a ball of less than 12 pounds.
I have been in a castle, besieged at the same
time by the enemy and battered with a shot of
18 pounds at near distance, which made but
a small dint in the stone walls thereof (viz. little
more than the concave side of a large deep
saucer) at every single shot. However, by repeated shots, the same or the very like cannons
did make a large breach (which I saw) in the like
walls elsewhere. I have seen the gates of a town
bored with many such shots, but not broken or
split. I stood by the cannonier when with an iron
gun under eight feet long, with a ball (as I guessed)
of seven or eight pounds at the most, he cleared
a road from the enemy's ships, which he sundry
times hit and harmed at a long mile's distance ; and
finally drove them away. Yet I looked sundry times
at the levelling of his cannon, and found it to be
mounted, when he made the best shots, much
above the hull of the ship even to the main-yard,
so that the gun could carry the bullet point blank
nothing near so far. One of these, removing full a
quarter of a mile further from the danger, did

afterwards shoot a random shot, armed with strong pikes, into the town from whence our cannon played, which shot came in through the back door of my house, where breaking through the door near the bottom, grazed on the floor, and raising itself again brake in pieces the pottage pot which was then actually in the hands of my maid servant, who was making the same clean. The maid received no harm, but one of the pikes was broken close off at the globe of the bullet, which was done, as I think, by the grazing, but we found it not. I think the round ball of this was about eight pound in weight. It flew near a mile and a half before it came to my house, which being armed (and consequently much hindered) by the pike or pikes abovesaid, was, as it seemed to me, a wonderful distance. I do think it probable that the gun of 28 pound, first above named, might, being mounted to its best height, send forth a random bullet five miles.

In my younger days I thought that the names of the poor husbandmen in our township did sound poorly, and to signify something contemptible even in the very sound. But I have lately

Nomina sive cognomina quædam in nostra vicinia.

observed my error and the cheats which custom
puts upon us; whereas I do rather now find that
many of those names are of great fame and
esteem, viz.—

| | |
|---|---|
| Marrow | Sir Wm. Marrow, Mayor of London, 34 Hen. VI. A valiant colonel slain in the King's service, 1644. |
| Barton | A famous Scotch commander, called Sir Andrew Barton. |
| Harrison | The late powerful rebel and regicide. |
| Williamson | Sir Joseph, a late Plenipotentiary and Secretary, 1676. |
| Ryce | A name in Wales most famous in our annals as princes or kings. |
| Griffith | Famous in the very same respect. |
| Howard | The chief name of English nobility. |
| Bullen | The name of an English Queen. |
| Hatton | The now Lord Hatton. |
| Ferrers | Anciently Earls of Derby |
| Stock | Said to be the name of the Emperors of the House of Austria. |

Joci.

Quibble, pun, punnet, pundigrion, of which
fifteen will not make up one single jest. I find

these words in Counsellor Manners' last legacy, printed 1676.

St. Ignatius advised the Provincials and other great officers in the Society of Jesus to be very attentive to the great and public affairs belonging to them, but not to meddle much in smaller matters. He said it was fitter that they should (fail to) correct others who erred in such small things than to lay themselves open by their own errors (which will be sure to happen oft if they meddle in small matters) to the censure or reprehension of inferior officers. And I think this is good advice even in worldiy affairs.

Observationes politicæ.

April 8, 1665.—Colonel Daniel, who had been a soldier for the Parliament and Commonwealth from about the beginning of the war and in many great employments, told me that during the whole time of his service on that side, which continued till the King came in, A.D. 1660, he never knew of any officers in their armies that ever fought in a single duel saving a corporal and a drummer. The corporal, having killed the drummer, was presently hanged at Edinborough, two regiments

Duellum.

being drawn up for that purpose. I hope it will not be denied that these armies consisted of valiant men.

Miracula.

I think it less damage to Christianity if we conceal a hundred true miracles, than if we publish one false one.

Convivia.

June 25, 1666.—I dined in the Castle at Dublin at the Lord Lieutenant's table. There were, besides the Duke and Duchess (Ormond), sixteen persons: we sat with our hats on. The first course had seventeen dishes, the second seventeen dishes, the third fifteen dishes, most of them choice sweet-meats. I had formerly dined there in the year 1662, and there was an excellent concert of instruments, the table being furnished much after the same manner as is above said. And I was told that it was his daily state and custom.

Minister cui tredecim uxores.

This present January 12, 1663, Major John Beversham told me that he was present at the Old Bailey when a minister (one Wilson, as I remember) was arraigned for having thirteen wives, and he was saved by his book, when another was hanged (for two wives) not being able to read. Quære, whether the book may be given in that case.

Although the life of man be most uncertain, yet do I not doubt at all but a far greater number of people grow up to old age than are commonly reported to do so. As a small instance of which I have observed that, within my memory (who am now this present year, 1660, forty years of age), no fewer than forty-three or forty-four persons at the least are counted of the inhabitants of Little Crosby, betwixt the Hall and the hill, who have lived about sixty years, and yet the number of houses are but twenty or thereabouts. *Longevi.*

Beat turrs (or old green gorse) in a tray till the pricks are rebated ; a beast or horse will eat them, and do as well as with hay. This I was told by Mr. Whittle of Kilkenny, an old soldier of Cromwell's. *Genista spinosa fit jumentorum pabulum.*

Feed sheep in the house with beans, ground round, and bran (with some oats if you will). Give them plenty of water and hay, and keep them warm. They will feed exceedingly fat in *Oves saginandæ.*

fourteen days. This is the practice in Flanders, where I learnt it. I suppose the winter is the chief time for this.

I did once make trial of this, but it did not succeed well. Yet it is most certainly and success-fully practised beyond the sea, as I was told at St. Omers by F. John Cary, the minister of the Eng-lish College, 1660.

Protestantes Anglicani.   The Duke of Buckingham, being asked by my Lady Castlemaine what religion he was of, an-swered that he had not faith enough to be a Pres-byterian, nor good works enough to be a Papist, and therefore he was an honest old Protestant without faith or good works. Mr. Anderton of Lostock told me this, August 11, 1669.

Commoda reipublicæ optanda.   It is a great damage in England, that it is held a shame for a man to do the offices of a woman in housewifery, as washing, milking, making cheese, butter, &c. In Flanders and Holland men do these things even much better than women, and very frequently. Here in England, seeing men are the best cooks, brewers, bakers and midwives, why should it be held a shame to milk, &c. ? The want of this causeth many men to marry fondly or to do worse, seeing they cannot (by reason of bad custom), keep house without a woman.

> It is now quite customary for men to milk, but they neither wash nor make butter ; cheese is no longer made in that part of Lancashire.

Keep rather too few than one too many, feed them well, and pay them with the most. *Servus et quomodo tractari debet.*

Adam Jovius, who writeth, thirteenth century, in the continuance of Baronius' Annals, speaking of the steeple at Argentine (Strasburg), A.D. 1277, saith it is 574 feet. The tower at St. Stephen's Church, Vienna, he affirms to be 480 feet high, and St. Paul's, in London (*e terrâ*), 534 : Our Lady's at Antwerp, 466. I did ascend the square steeple at Durham, A.D. 1634, and I counted the steps to be between sixteen and seventeen score, which are more than the steps of St. Paul's in London, there being between fifteen and sixteen score to the top of the square steeple which I ascended in 1638. Yet there were at Durham upon the same church two spires at the west end (besides two less spires at the east end), which were leaded on the outside and were much higher than the *Turres altiores.*

square.   But one of them being fallen of late years, I hear that the other is taken down (1664).   In 1660, I counted the steps of the steeple of St. Martin's Church at Ipres to be 342, containing more than six inches a piece.   Upon this steeple is a spire, which I did ascend by twenty-five larger steps.   I ascended St. John's steeple at Gant (1660), by 426 steps of seven inches at the least. Upon the square top of this there is a tower to be ascended by thirty steps more, but I did not ascend that.

I counted the steps of Nôtre Dame in Paris to be 250, so far as I could well ascend, for the height was much more, these 250 reaching even with the top of the church.

On July 8, 1666, I ascended St. Patrick's steeple in Dublin by 176 steps of an unequal height, which I take to be (at a medium) $7\frac{3}{4}$ inches.

Sentent'æ
morales.

He that has too much of a good fellow, has too little of a good Christian.

Agricultura.

The improvement of land by marl, where timber did lately grow, is well known to be exceeding great.   Sir William Gerard told me

(March 11, 1662), that Mr. Leigh, having marled sundry acres where Haydock wood stood, has farmed the same for 4*l.* 10*s.* and for 5*l.* the acre yearly for the term of ten years. Sir William Gerard told me at the same time, that he himself hath two acres of such improved wood land, which hath yielded him 120 bushels of barley yearly upon each acre. He told me likewise then, that he had land which hath at some times yielded 140 bushels by the acre.

I have a book which is entitled ' Opusculum de regimine rusticorum.' It seems to be a notable piece. It is said that if you put seed corn into a sack which hath lately been filled with meal, the meal not being well dusted out, that the said seed when sown will produce pitiful dwindling corn. *Uredinem Contrahit.* This was told me by Hamlet Massey, who noted it out of ' Kerkerous ' Sympathies.

'Tis surely a far less deplorable spectacle to see a gentleman spoiled of his fortune by his conscience than his luxury, and to behold him under the stroke of the headsman, than under those more infamous executioners, his lust or intemperance. *Nobiles parum nobiles.*

Shall those, who have not so much Christian patience as to bear the slightest reproach for God, have yet so much unchristian stupidity as to endure the greatest in opposition to Him? Those that consume all on hawks, hounds, and horses, seem to make the same menace to their estates which Goliath did to David: 'I will give thee to the fowls of the air, and to the beasts of the field.'

Carmina incondita.

Sir Vivian Molyneux told me of two verses written over the gate of the Savoy at London; which are (as I remember), these—

King Henry the Seventh, to his worship and honour,
Builded this hospital, poor people to succour.

Sir Vivian Molyneux, born November 1, 1595, was fourth son of Sir Richard Molyneux, who was created Bart. in 1611, the first year of such creations, and was brother to Richard, the first Viscount Molyneux. Anthony-a-Wood says of him : 'He travelled into several foreign countries, was at Rome where (tho' puritanically educated under the tuition of Sam Radcliffe of Brazen-nose College, Oxford), he changed his religion, returned a well-bred man, was knighted, and in the grand rebellion suffered for the royal cause. He translated from Spanish into English "A treatise of the difference between the Temporal and Eternal," London, 1672, October, wrote originally by G. Eusebius Nieremberg, S. J.' (Fasti

i. 346). He was admitted amongst the students of the English College, Rome, as a 'convictor' or boarder, on September 29, 1617, under the name of Thomas Leigh.—J. E. B.

The best cure for a flux of blood is supposi- *Hibernici morbi cu-* tories made of the fat of hung bacon, put up be- *ratio.* twixt every stool till you find the effect, which will be complete in two days. If the bacon be reasted, it is rather better than otherwise. This was told me by my old kind friend Mr. Price, the Protestant Bishop of Kildare, who had good experience of it.

I take flattery not to be that common and *Adulatio.* harmless faculty of good language and plausible address, but a diabolical art of holding intelligence with natural corruption and accommodating itself to our vices whatsoever they be.

She was the wife of Judge P. of Wales, a *P. Donin..* woman of an incomparable wit, but fondly be- sotted of her children. When her eldest son was in the cradle, she would not permit either geese, hogs, or any such like things to be kept about the house, lest their noise should wake the child. The magpies were persecuted for that reason with a gun up and down the demesne. Her indulgence in other things was ridiculously suited to this. Witness her standing with the child to delight him with the creaking of an old gate, whilst they lost the sermon at the church to which they were going. When this son of hers was sent to the University, he had a maid along with him to attend him. After, when the mother lay desperately sick, the gratitude of the children appeared. For her sons (otherwise immeasurably disrespectful), drank up in contempt the ale that was brewed for their mother, and ranted so loud in the next room to hers, that she sent to require their silence. Whereupon they doubled their noise, with shouts and horns, and dogs and horses, brought for that end into a ground chamber where they were, by trampling and howling to fright away their mother's soul. She died, indeed, soon after, and even at the last gasp confessed her fond indulgence to have been the cause of her own greatest grief and her children's wickedness. Since her death they do frequently make mention of her in this manner, ' That w—e, my mother.' When the Judge, their father, lay upon his deathbed (whereupon he had lain as a languishing man for many months), this his eldest son would reproach him with these words : ' Oh thou old wicked rogue, now do despair and the pains of hell seize on thy cursed soul for such and such faults in thy younger days.' These things I heard from Mr. George Fo. and Mrs. P. a Welsh woman, 1659. And no doubt much more no less horrid might be learned of others. And other things I have heard since, October 6, 1660.

> In a letter to Laurence Ireland, dated November 22, 1667, Mr. Blundell gives the following account of the miserable end of the eldest of these unnatural children :—
> ' Mr. P. of Flintshire, the great heir of the Judge of that name, lost his life by the same excess, concerning whom alone I could write a history, which might fright all the parents in the world from being too fond of their children.'

John Bradshaw, the President who condemned King Charles I., was the younger son of one Bradshaw, called Goodman of Cheshire. Mr. Raphael Hollinshead told me that, being a boy at the school, he made certain English rhymes in contention (as it were) with his brother, some of which ran thus—

*Bradshawus sceleratus.*

Harry thou art, and thou must to the plough and
cart,
But I am John, that honour must attend upon.

John Bradshaw the Regicide was the youngest
son of Henry Bradshaw, Esq., of Marple Hall,
County Cheshire, four miles from Stockport. The
property is still held by a descendant in the female
line. The verses said to have been scratched by
the President, when a boy, upon a tombstone, are
elsewhere differently given, but the above version,
resting as it does on the authority of a Cheshire
man, a relative and namesake of the famous Chroni-
cler, is probably correct.

1663.—Lords esteemed to be Catholics who are
Peers of the Realm :

Marquises—Winchester, Worcester, Dorchester.

Earls—Bristol, Cardigan, Shrewsbury, Norwich,
Rivers.

Lords—Andover, Abergavenny, Arundel of
Wardour, Teynham, Langdale, Stourton, Went-
worth, Barkley, Montague, Carrington, Powis,
Crofts, Bellasis, Vaux, Audley (Earl of Castlehaven), Petre, Stafford.

Catholic Lords not Peers of the Realm—

Dunbar, Molineux, Fairfax, Baltimore, Lumley.

In this list Mr. Blundell seems to have omitted
some Irish and Scotch Peers who were Catholics,

and on the other hand, to have represented as Catholics some English Peers who were not really so. Taking the list as it stands, we find only five of the above peerages held by Catholic descendants. For the sake of comparison we give a complete list of Catholic Peers at the present time (1880) :—

Duke—Norfolk.

Marquises—Bute, Ripon.

Earls—Denbigh, Newburgh, Westmeath, Fingal, Granard, Ashburnham, Kenmare, Orford, Gainsborough.

Viscounts—Gormanston, Netterville, Taaffe, Southwell.

Barons—Mowbray and Stourton, Camoys, Beaumont, Vaux, Petre, Arundel of Wardour, Dormer, Stafford, Clifford, Ashford, Herries, Lovat, Louth, French, Bellew, De Freyne, Howard of Glossop, Acton, O'Hagan, Emly, Gerard, Braye.

Of these, twenty-nine only are Peers of the Realm, against twenty-five in the preceding list. It will be noticed how very little remains of the old element in the present Catholic peerage after the lapse of two centuries. No fewer than twelve of the peers above enumerated are converts to the Catholic faith. When the comparative small number of peers in 1663 is taken into account, it will be seen that a much larger proportion of peers was Catholic at that period than at the present day. At the same time it must be remembered that from the time of James II. to the end of the reign of George IV. (a period of 150 years), no Catholic received the distinction of a peerage, although the creations during that period were very numerous. Lingard gives the

list of Catholic Peers excluded from the House of
Lords by the Bill of 1678 as follows :—

Duke—Norfolk.

Marquis—Worcester.

Earls—Shrewsbury, Berkshire, Portland, Cardigan, Powis.

Viscounts—Montague, and Stafford.

Barons—Mowbray, Audley, Stourton, Petre,
Arundel, Hunsdon, Belasyse, Langdale, Teynham,
Carrington, Widdrington, Gerard of Bromley, Clif-
ford.

*Anglicè*
*scribendi*
*modus*

The Rhemes Testament is bad English. I
heard that Sir Toby Matthew, reading the title
page, 'The New Testament, &c., faithfully translated into English," said it was a lie, for it was not
English.

Bugle notes
for the hunt.

To call the companie in the morninge.

The strake to the feeilde is seven.

When the hounds be uncupled—the seeke.

When the hounds doe hunt a game unknowne.

When the hounds have found the game—the rechaite.

The strake of eight to drawe from the covert.

The yearthinge of a fox if hee bee coverable.

If he be not coverable—the call away.

The death of a fox in feild or covert.

The calls for a keeper in parke or forrest.

The death of a bucke with bowe or grayhound.

The death of bucke in parke or forrest.

The prise of a harte rial with the rechaite.

The strake of nine to call home the companie.

The strake of five for the tarrears.

The mount is from parte to parte, and curricall three repeated.

The long rechaite.

JOHN SCOTT.

SIR R. BRADSHAIGH.

This seems to have been inserted in 'Hodge-podge' by Sir Roger Bradshaigh. John Scott was his huntsman.

Wainscot.

1664, May 7.—The wainscot of my dining room being finished, we measured the same, and found it, without the chimney corner, to be 109 yards 2 feet. And the lining of the great door cheeks were, although plain work, accounted as wainscot. The plane tier and the crest were reckoned (measuring not perpendicular but slope-wise) to 7 inches high or broad. And the cusitooses (besides the rail on which they stand) were measured at

2 inches high. So that the whole work was 11 feet 11 inches high. My bargain was to have all the panels cloven timber except the frize and the lowest course. But yet there were fifteen or twenty panellings of sawed wood, contrary to bargain. I was to pay 3*s*. 7*d*. a yard for all, and if I liked the work, 2*d*. more. The work I did like and paid for—

|  | £ | *s.* | *d.* |
|---|---|---|---|
| 109 yards 2 feet . . . . . | 17 | 6 | 0 |
| The man with whom I bargained, made the pilasters upon his own account, for which I gave him 4*s*., which 4*s*. he gave to the labourer, an honest workman, who made all with the help of a boy or two in short time . | 0 | 4 | 0 |
| I gave this labourer at several times 8*s*. and to his son 3*s*. . . . . | 0 | 11 | 0 |
| All the nails which were used cost me about . . . . . . | 0 | 3 | 0 |

I had a mason three days to make holes for the wood to be put, unto which we pinned it. The joiner and his boy were working seven days in putting up the wainscot. I only gave them meat. I take this wainscot to be the cheapest

D D

great work which I have done about my house, and I think it was the only great thing in all my expenseful work which did fall short, in charge, of my expectation.

Epistolæ. Mr. Loveday's letters are esteemed by many to be most quaint and ingenious, but it seems to me as if they were of that number, which Ben Jonson saith go a-begging to be understood. The expressions, indeed, are nothing vulgar, but the sense is as plain as may be. For an example of which I do propose, that one of the choice epistles be translated out of that new-fashioned English phrase into plain honest English, and I think it will then look like a plucked peacock. And the like may be done to show the worthless gaudiness of many other writings.

A good character adds much to a well-indited letter, but the faults of an ill-indited letter are much hid by a character which is not easily read. My physician [Dr. Worthington of Wigan—Ed.] wrote unto me most material prescriptions in time of my great danger by sickness. I showed these unto three most expert readers, and neither they nor I could read it, or understand the main points of the letter. I told the writer how ill he had done therein. He answered that the letter was so plainly written, that there was never a boy in Wigan school unto whom the same was not legible.

Captain Tarleton shot a right good musket, *Globus tor-mentarius.* with a charge and a half of powder, at a full bag of wool (about twenty stone). He stood about nine yards off it, and shot quite through it and next an inch and a half into a door behind it. He told me this, and showed me the hole in the door. And he said that he saw one shoot a musket, at thirty yards distance, at a bag of cotton (which is very hard and close). He shot not through it, but the cotton appeared thrust out by the bullet, like a finger, on the other side.

The verse 'Alexandrine' consists of twelve or *Anglice scribendi modus.* thirteen syllables. This I take to be the way of our old English poets, and particularly in the old translation of 'Virgil,' where the second book be-gins thus—

They whisted all, and fixt with eyes attentive did
    behold
Where Lord Æneas from high bench thus he told.

Thomas Phaer translated 'Virgil,' A.D. 1555, being moved thereunto for the defence of his country's language, which he had heard discommended. What a silly piece of English this is may be judged by the reader.

R. Willes writes a preface to Peter Martir's 'Decades of the West Indies,' translated by R. Eden, printed in London, 1577. Willes says, 'Many of his English words cannot be excused in my opinion for smelling too much of the Latin, as, ponderous, antiques, despicable, obsequious, homicide, destructive, prodigious, &c.' These words are now common (1690).

*Zealotypia.*

Jealousy is a bad daughter born of a good house.

*Conjuges quales esse debent inter se.*

Let the married couple, when they consult together upon occasion of differences with others, carry themselves justly, lest by teaching each other how to wrong a third person, they be instructed, as conscious of their own mutual knowledges, to be unjust to themselves.

It is accounted a piece of ill-breeding to see a man go abroad with his own wife. ('Ladies'

Calling,' pt. ii. page 30). I suppose those who brought up these rules are not to seek what use to make of them.

When I was at Paris in the month of August and September 1681, I received there from Sir John Warner a catalogue of the names of the English Jesuits, the total number whereof in all places, living or supposed to be living 23rd May 1681, was just 280, viz., Fathers 174 (69 professed), and brothers 106. Of this number there were then at Liege 16 fathers and 59 brothers, students, &c. ; in all 75. In England there were 109, of whom four were lay brothers. The rest were at St. Omers, Ghent, Watten, Spain, &c.

*Jesu Societas Anglicana.*

The Rev. Sir John Warner of Parham, Suffolk, Bart., had a romantic history. He married in 1659 Miss Trevor Hanmer, daughter of Sir Thomas Hanmer of Hanmer, Flintshire, Bart., and had this title conferred on himself in 1660 for his loyal and faithful services. Lady Warner and Elizabeth Warner, a sister of Sir John's, became converts to the Catholic faith in 1664. Sir John being inclined the same way consulted Dr. Buck, who had been his grandfather's chaplain, and afterwards called on the Archbishop of Canterbury (Dr. Sheldon). The latter handed him over to Dr. Dolbin, Dean of Westminster, who told him that it was a mere

punctilio the Pope stood upon, which hindered the
union of the two churches.   Sir John Warner, not
being satisfied, ended his doubts by entering the
Catholic Church.   He and his Lady then agreed to
part for the purpose of embracing a religious life.
Sir John, after providing for his two children, settled
his estate on his next brother Francis, and entered
the Novitiate, S.J., at Watten, under the name of
Clare.   Here he ' divided the commons,' to use Mr.
Blundell's expression, with Laurence Ireland of
Lydiate, Esq., who had lately taken the very same
step, and who wrote to his friend about this time, a
full account of the conversion of Sir John Warner.
In 1667, his brother Francis came over to see him,
and having been in the mean time converted, felt
the same longing for a religious life.   Having visited
Nieuport, where there was a colony of Carthusians,
he admired their strict way of life and resolved to
embrace it.   In his eagerness to return to England,
to settle his affairs before carrying out this design,
he urged the captain of the vessel on which he had
taken his passage to set sail, although the weather
was threatening.   Overcome by his promises, the ship
was put to sea, and had scarcely left the port when
she encountered a terrible gale and became a complete wreck.   Francis Warner was drowned within
sight of the monastery where he had hoped to pass
his days, and was interred as one of their brethren
by the Carthusian monks.   Sir John Warner, hearing
of the sad occurrence, and having his estate once
more fallen to him, was obliged to undertake a
journey to London, where he found a second
brother Edmund, on whose not unwilling shoulders
he laid his burthen.   After his ordination Sir John

spent most of his life abroad, but was in England in
the office of Provincial, S.J., from 1689 to 1693.
He died at Watten in 1705. Lady Warner died a
Poor Clare at Gravelines in 1670, and her two
daughters ended their days as Benedictine Nuns at
Dunkirk. The Cavalier's grandson, Nicholas Blundell, relates that Sir John Warner had in his younger
days been passionately fond of hawking, and that
once, when he happened to be at Dunkirk, a tame
hawk which had been caught was brought to him.
On examining it Sir John discovered by certain
secret marks that it was his own hawk which had
flown out of Suffolk. The life of Lady Warner of
Parham was published in London in 1692. (See
Foley's 'Records, S.J.' vol. ii.) Laurence Ireland
adds to the above particulars, that the estate which
Sir John Warner resigned was of the value of 800*l.*
per annum, and that he was twenty-six years of age
when he made this sacrifice.

Peter Blundell of Tiverton, clothier, erected a Blundell.
fair free school in that town, and allowed it a competent maintenance and lodgings for a master and
usher. He bestowed two scholarships and two
fellowships on Sidney College, Cambridge, providing Tiverton scholars should be elected therein.
'Tis thought he died about 1596. In the Paris
' Gazette,' January 26, 1686, I found this :—

January 22. 'Le sieur Blondell, Maréchal des
Camps et Armées du Roy, Professeur Royal des

Mathématiques, de l'Académie Royale des Sciences, et ci-devant Maistre des Mathématiques de Monseigneur le Dauphin, mourut ici après une longue maladie. Il avait été Envoyé du Roy à Constantinople, et il avait fait pour le service de sa Majestie divers voyages en Levant, en Afrique, en Amérique et en plusieurs cours de l'Europe. Il s'étoit acquitté de tous ces différents emplois avec une grande capacité.' This man hath published many learned writings.

I found at London a good number of Blundells, viz.: a considerable merchant at his house near London Stone. One Richard Blundell, an ingenious young man and surgeon, lived near Bishopsgate Street, westward from it and in some close buildings. There was then an Attorney of good note who frequented the coffee-houses in and about Gerard Street. Another attorney of good parts (yet somewhat blemished by good fellowship), in one of the Inns below Holborn Bar, who had a brother of the same name, living in or very near Bloomsbury Market. He has the repute of a very ingenious man, and is said to keep at the joiners' trade about eighteen or twenty servants. Mr. Thomas Morton, silkman, told me, about the year

1687, that one Blundell in the city, a plain, clownish man, had gained an estate by weaving laces, of above 1,000*l.* per annum. I think he told me that the weaver was lately dead, and that the son was a very well-bred and genteel person.

I have writing, which came under the Privy Seal of King Henry II., where my antecessor N. B. is written Nicholas Blondell, Esq.

A.D. 1681.—There are in Paris three Academies, in all which the learner's expense is equal— viz. 1,300 livres for his diet, exercise, and lodging ; for a Governor's diet and lodging, 600 livres ; for a servant's diet and lodging, 300 livres. The six masters (if you use them), each of them a louis d'or or one pistole at your entrance—viz. for dancing, fencing, geography, mathematics, pike and musket, and when first you ride the ring. Thirty sols per mensem for switches, and as much for music. Some few half-crowns a year to other officers. It is a question whether besides all this you be not charged to pay for the furniture of your chamber. I rather think you are not. All this is besides apparell for yourself and servants. If you will lodge in the town, you may exercise

*Academia Parisiensis.*

E E

riding in the Academy at four pistoles per mensem, but no other exercise. Those in the Academy may stay as little a while as they please, and the advance will be refunded. The expense of Academies out of Paris amounts to a full third part less, the charge for diet, exercise, and lodging being but 800 francs.

Judicia in
Catholico-
rum hostes.

I read in the great English Chronicle at Croxteth, September 10, 1660, of great punishments that happened to those that had a chief hand in the subversion of the forty monasteries, granted by Pope Clement VII. to Cardinal Wolsey. Of those five men which were chiefly employed by the Cardinal about it, two fought with each other : one of them was killed and the other hanged for it. A third drowned himself. Another, that was a bishop in Ireland, became sadly lamed, and the fifth, that was formerly a rich man, died a beggar. The Pope suffered by the loss of Rome, &c., and the King and Cardinal as we know.

I have heard of a part of England (either Norfolk or Northampton, as I take it), wherein it is observed by a Protestant writer of note, that within a small compass or tract of land there lived about twenty gentlemen, consisting all or in part of religious lands. About as many lived in the same tract whose estates had no part of any such lands. It was noted that, whereas there was but one or two of this second sort that had come to ruin or any notable decay since Henry VIII., there were but one or two of the first sort that had 'skaped from such ruin. I believe Mr. Edwards, *alias* Anderton, can say something to this business.

The horrid judgments upon sequestrators, committee men and farmers of Catholic estates, have been remarkable. Quære, of Mr. Chorley and his daughters' disastrous ends. And note those incomparable disasters upon Mr. Moore's family, since Edward Moore, about the year 1632, fell dead upon the road. He was a great persecutor, &c.

Spelman is the writer of note referred to above.

Soon cry, soon dry. See how mourning and tears are commended at funerals, as it were for fashion's sake and to satisfy others. Lacrymæ.

A curious person who spends two much time in reading, may be said to be ignorant of almost Curiosi.

nothing, his own misery and weakness only ex-
cepted. If we ask him for whom he labours, he
will tell you, ' I read to please myself.' This upon
the whole is no more than to please a roving fancy,
and it is very well for him if he do not regret it
when repentance comes too late. A man may be
too covetous of knowledge as well as of coin, and
whether he stands possessed of the one or the other
without making advantage of them for himself and
his neighbour, it is like to cost him dear when the
account is made.

L'Estrange, Roger.

In his ' Observator,' No. 5, February 19, 1684–5,
in answer to Trimmer, who taxes him with med-
dling too much about Oates' miscarriage, he says :

' I entered upon this commission by the order
of his late sacred Majesty of ever blessed memory.
I continued my proceedings upon it by the same
Royal and repeated commands, and if it had not
been for some previous deliberations in what
manner to proceed and which causes to pitch
upon out of the choice of eleven or twelve, this
matter had been brought to an issue time enough
for the late King to have seen this wretched creature
brought to public shame and justice. . . . I must

avow further that his Majesty was pleased to declare this scrutiny to be a point highly incumbent on his Royal justice. Thus I began, thus I proceeded, and by the grace of God thus I resolve to continue, till I see this point brought to a conclusion. Having the honour of his present Majesty's commission, also to prosecute the orders and intentions of the late King.'

I saw (in 1658) an old hollow oak close by the road betwixt London and Tunbridge, wherein (as I was then assured) 140 boys were placed, who all came swarming out of it unexpectedly to entertain King James with admiration, as he passed that way on hunting.

*Arbores in-gentiores.*

Mr. Ireland of Lydiate told me, that he saw an oak that grows in the forest of Delamere, the bole of which is affirmed to be in circumference 14 yards. Mr. Henry Stanley told me at the same instant that the said oak was measured to be in circumference about the bole 14 yards 1 foot. This they told me October 2, 1663.

When I was about nine years old, my grandfather Blundell showed me the oak in the north corner of the new orchard, and making me to clip it

about, I found that my finger ends did overreach
each other some little, less than an inch I take it. He
told me, that he did plant that tree when it was
like a small twig which he showed me (less than
ordinary riding rod). And now this present December 18, 1663, I being in the 44th year of
my age, I measured the same tree again, clipping
it in my arms as high as I could well reach, standing on the west side, and I found it to be 9 inches
(within less than one straw's breadth) more than I
could fathom. My grandfather was born 1560.

*Antichristus.*      Mr. Samuel Aspinwall, a zealous puritan of a
moral conversation, talking with me this day
(February 13, 1663) as he hath often done, professed that if he did not think the Pope were Anti-
christ, he would turn Papist. 'For if he be not
so,' saith he, 'we cannot excuse ourselves from
schism.'

*Eleemo-*
*synæ.*      The same old beggar whom I have mentioned
before used to beg in a rhetorical bold way at the
races on Crosby marsh, and he would flatter the
noble gentlemen, and tell aloud what gallant
houses they kept. His importunity there was in-

sufferable. I did there once see a gentleman cast
a shilling unto him, saying, 'A pox o' God take
thee!' The boldest wandering beggars (and a
Bedlam one, Medcalf, above all others) ever speeded
the best at these races, whilst the truly poor
widows and orphans who lived in the parish found
little effect there of their modest low way of begging. Tom Arnold told me that he saw at night
near that place thirty or forty of these wandering
beggars at Rogerson's (a paltry alehouse), spending the money they had gotten at the race.

April 21, 1676.—This day my servants did
shear eight wethers unwashed, and weighed (*me
ipso vidente*) the fleeces of the same, the weight of
which was fully sixty pounds, whereof five pounds
was foul-knotted wool. One of these eight fleeces,
without any knotted wool, weighed eight pounds
fully. These were Irish sheep, part of forty-six
which I had bought for 23*l.* the last June, and I did
shear the same afterwards (1675), so that these
last fleeces wanted much of a year's growth. Note
that I had sold twenty choice sheep out of the
forty-six aforesaid, and afterwards ten choice sheep,
so that six or seven of the abovesaid eight sheep

*Lana appensa.*

were as it were the refuse of the forty-six. After the wool aforesaid had been washed and dried it weighed (as my wife told me) but forty-five pounds.

Anglicè loquendi modus.

It think it is probable that the false pronunciation of many words hath first arisen through a childish error in reading. For example, the word 'through' is but one syllable, and yet it is now commonly pronounced, especially by the nicer sort, as if it were of two syllables. The word 'ask' is called by many 'axe' by a mistake (I conceive) in reading. 'Massacre' (I take it) is called 'massacar' by the like mistake. But custom in this is a law. I have heard sundry gentlewomen, who were good readers of English, pronounce the word 'anxiety' as if it had been writ 'anexety.' And who can doubt but if that word were very commonly mistaken in the same manner, it might in the end exchange its own essence? We may add the words 'sure' and 'sugar,' which are commonly pronounced 'shure' and 'shuggar.'

We may observe that many Englishmen, who are great scholars and have spent their time abroad, are very defective and oftentimes ridiculous (although they will hardly believe it) in their English tongue. I heard one of these in a sermon repeat the name of a certain precious stone (unto the rare virtues of which he did piously allude) no fewer than twenty times. And yet the name of this stone did sound as filthily in our language, as any word whatsoever in the English tongue. What strange apprehensions would the ruder sort of people frame hereupon ?

An amusing incident of this nature happened a few years ago in a neighbouring town. A youth had been sent to Louvaine from a country district in Ireland to study for the Priesthood. Here he soon acquired the language of his new companions, and made good progress in his studies. In due time he was ordained Priest, and came home a well educated and polished man. On landing in England he was asked to preach to a mixed congregation of English and Irish. He had no difficulty in preparing an excellent discourse, but found that he had no language wherewith to clothe his ideas excepting that of his boyhood. As may well be imagined, his thoroughly Irish manner and the droll expressions which he used had an irresistibly comic effect.

Women may pretend a little to govern because Fæmina audax. men have governed so ill, as plausibly as some have reformed the Church upon the like pretence.

F F

Heidelber-
gensis cadus.

Concerning the great tun of Heidelberg mentioned by Ben Jonson and by other English poets, I did enquire of a German whom I met in France and of a Frenchman who travelled in our company, and one of them affirmed that it did contain 300 wain-loads of wine, which was no less, said the other, than 2,800 French hogsheads or dolia. Both of these gentlemen had seen the said tun and they were very sober men.

Pendrel,
Richard.

King Charles II. in his flight from Worcester, 1651, was cast by his nobles (by the Earl of Derby) upon the care and fidelity of Richard Pendrel, a poor Catholic in leathern breeches. And Catholics were many of them the sole instruments of his safety at the first brunt.

Literæ ab-
stergendæ
vel renovan-
dæ.

Boil galls in wine, and with a sponge wipe over the letters. They will presently be seen when they are once wet, and be well coloured as they were at first. Aquafortis in a feather (or a sponge) held near to the letters will exhale the ink to it. John Wilson saith that one Mr. Denby, a stationer at Warrington, useth it.

Dictum
Reginæ
Hispaniæ de
Jesuita.

This was the wife of Philip III., who was a singular great friend to the Jesuits. It chanced

that one of that order in Spain had committed
some kind of fault, which came immediately to
the King's ear. Whereupon the King, going in all
haste to the Queen, related the story, and asked
(by way of reproach) what she could say now in
excuse of the Jesuits. The Queen returned this
sudden and witty reply : ' Sir, I can nothing say in
defence of those fathers but this—that (without
all question) the bell that sounds so loud with so
small a touch must needs be of an excellent temper.' *Narravit mihi*, Pater Richd. Banester, Provs.
Ord. in Angliâ, 1660.

I do not remember that any capital crime, but <sub>Duellum.</sub>
this of duels, is frequently and publicly defended
by persons otherwise discreet and sober. The
women (or young girls) do urge on the men by
crying that down for cowardice, which God and
the laws command. And this the giglets do, because it is not the mode in the romances for
gentlemen to refuse a challenge. I knew a youth
in the fourteenth year of his age, with whom I had
great means to be acquainted ; but I found him
reserved and unwilling to talk (though I tried him
in sundry ways and on many subjects), until I

chanced to speak of the point of honour and duels.
You cannot believe how far he was transported
with this discourse.  To show how deeply he was
possessed with it at that age, he gave me a spon-
taneous account of the most remarkable actions
of that nature in the country where he lived, and
seemed able to give a list both of the swordsmen
and the cowards.  This I conceived was occasioned
by the discourse which he heard from his father,
who was ever a great deal too forward in the mistaken points of honour.  How far did boys and
girls who were martyred in the primitive Church
exceed these swashbucklers in valour!  There were
no parasites or pot companions to extoll them ;
they were wounded on all hands as well by words
as by blows.

The young man referred to was no doubt one of
his grandsons, a son of Viscount Mountgarret, who
had married Mr. Blundell's eldest daughter Emilia.

See a story in the fifteenth book of Davila, his
' French Civil Wars,' where the Sieur de Coquein
Villiar, one of the King's servants, gave a box on
the ear to Monsieur de Bonivet in the King's ante-
chamber ; for which Coquein Villiar acknowledged
his fault and offered to ask his pardon, refusing a

challenge which Bonivet sent unto him, and keeping himself in-doors to avoid the duel. At last, being forced to fight, he killed Bonivet and had the King's pardon and favour. This is noted as well for the worthy satisfaction offered for striking a man where he durst not defend himself, as for the King's great moderation in pardoning a gentleman who, being surprised with the apprehension of losing his own honour, forgets his duty to his sovereign, and doth yet upon that occasion afterwards show both great submission and valour.

Take a kite and a carrion crow, and tie them down in the stubble with sufficient liberty, and they will fight and cry in a strange manner; upon which there will come immediately great flocks of crows from all parts, which striking freely at the kite will many of them be taken in the lime twig which must be placed round in the stubble for that reason. Remember that you tie up one foot of your kite to make the battle more equal. You may easily take a kite with a pigeon and lime. The dun horny kite is thought to be the best.

*Aucupium et variæ ejus artes.*

Set many lime twigs in a tree, growing in a wood, the boughs many of the smallest being first cut off. Then betake yourself to a bower under the tree, a good while after sunset. There, with an owl-call made with a hazel, you may call a world of birds about you, pyes, jays, thrushes, &c., which will hop up and down, and many of them be taken with the twigs. Your dog or yourself may fetch them in. October is the best time for this sport.

If you take a quick and lively magpie, and lay her on the ground upon her back in such sort that her wings be fastened to the earth, the stir and noise she will make will call many other magpies about her which lighting upon her (as it were to succour or relieve her), she will hold the first that comes fast with her claws, till you may come and take her. This you may pin down by the other in like manner, and so you may do until you have taken a great number of those birds. The best time for this is when they pair.

Take waterfowl with hooks baited with the lites of a beast, which is a flesh that will swim. The above experiment with a magpie has been tried successfully by Mr. Thomas Stanton, from whom I had it.

Stadium
Crosbiense.

This course, as it is now used upon the marshes of Great and Little Crosby, was stooped out by me

W. B., A.D. 1654, at the request of Richard Lord
Molyneux. I did not then, nor have I yet
measured it (1663). Only I caused my man to
pace over the first mile of the old course of Liverpoole (which standeth partly even with a part of
Crosby course), and I find that from the stone
where the first mile ends to anenst Crosby stoop, is
contained 35 rods of 8 yards. To anenst the stoop
in the Gorse, 125, and to the ending stones, 237
and 3 yards. This mile (and the whole course of
Liverpoole), which seemeth not to agree with the
measure in use, was set out by my father. From
the end of this mile to the plat, 27 rods. From
the plat to the starting pole on the Morehouse
marsh, 116 rods and 4 yards. But note that these
measures are not to be relied on till further trial.

In or about the year 1683, I procured a great
change in this course, viz. that the starting place
(which was also the end of the course) having been
formerly on the Morehouse marsh, it was then
changed to that pole or corner of the said course
which stands on Great Crosby marsh, about 30
yards from the sandy fence or doles which separate
the marsh from the holme. This is now (1686-7)
both the beginning and the end of the course.

Ben
Jonson.

See his ' Discoveries,' where he speaks of the envy towards an able writer who shall be better understood in another age. He showeth his abilities to be such, as if he hath given a character of himself (page 100). Ben Jonson's head is put up for a sign in London and sundry places.

The above passage has been generally supposed to refer to Shakespeare, of whose writings Mr. Blundell appears to have known little. (See Introductory Chapters).

Wolves and
drunkards.

Drunkards and other sensual persons may be considered, in reference to the number of sober and virtuous men, as wolves are considered with sheep. Wolves are produced in multitudes, five or six at a litter. Sheep, but one by one. Wolves destroy sheep. Sheep destroy no wolves. Sheep in great multitudes do yield their lives and blood, and suffer themselves to be shorn and even exenterated without the least resistance, for man's behoof. Whereas wolves, by all dexterous arts of force and craft, avoid the sight of man, are rarely entrapped, and doing much mischief to the world, do very seldom pay for it with the loss of their lives. Then how comes it to pass, that the number of wolves increases not to be infinitely more than the number of sheep? which we see to be much otherwise. It is answered truly that wolves, however they join oft in mischief, do frequently kill and devour each other, and by that sole means do disburthen the world in a great measure of their mischief. The application of these things is very obvious.

Lerpoole had three *Lord* Mayors not four years since, Then an honest tradesman, and now a prince.

Richmond Silvester, Maior of Leverpoole.

These three lords were the Earl of Derby, Lord Colchester, and Lord Strange. The townsman was Mr. Bicsteth. Dr. Richmond is called a prince by reason of his noble way of living. This was writ 1673.

Dr. Richmond resided at Thornton Hall in the immediate neighbourhood of Crosby. The property is still held by the family, and its present representative has his residence near the old mansion.

1664.—I concluded to pay 1*l.* 5*s.* the thousand for hewing and filling, and to brew three bushels of malt into small beer for hewers and fillers, and two bushels for strong beer for all the workmen. The carters were to have 2*s.* 6*d.* per day and no meat for their horses. The whole sum of loads I do ac-

Marling the higher Oaklands.

G G

count to be 5,180, and the workmen do account the loads to be 5,200.

| | £ | s. | d. |
|---|---|---|---|
| After which account I have paid them . | 6 | 10 | 0 |
| And I do account for carts hired . . | 6 | 0 | 0 |
| And for my own carts at 2s. 6d. per day | 1 | 12 | 0 |
| For fourteen days' spreading with two men . . . . . . . | 1 | 9 | 8 |
| For a water-bearer at 7d. for fourteen days . . . . . . . | 0 | 8 | 9 |
| Total . . . . | 16 | 0 | 5 |
| I do moreover conjecture that the feying of the pit cost about . . . . | 2 | 4 | 7 |

My wife sent the workmen 5s. when their own small beer was ending, and bade them choose whether they would have that or else a supply of small beer till the end of the work. They chose the latter, and I believe all our beer given by bargain or otherwise from first to last was worth 1l. 2s., which with a little tobacco, &c., and a poor accidental dinner on Saturday when they had ended, may be accounted . . . . . . 1 5 0

So that the total charge was . . £19 10 0

I guess the land to be somewhat considerably less than four acres. The hewing and filling, at 1*l.* 5*s.* per thousand, cost one farthing per load. The men had about 16*s.* as I take it in gifts from my friends.

It is no small victory for reason to overcome the senses. And it may appear the greater, if we do well consider how long the senses have domineered in us (during our whole infancy and childhood) with little or no opposition at all of our reason. Let me judge of the far different powers of sense and reason by this one example. Upon the first or second sight of the skull of a dear friend of mine who died many years before, my reason hath been so convinced concerning the vanity of wit, beauty, and other worldly blessings (whereof my dear friend had enjoyed a great share), that I have very seldom been more disposed to goodness and more adverse to vanity than at that time. And yet, upon the frequent renewing of the same object, I have looked upon it at the last as if I had only looked on a painted skull. But now on the other side, where sense hath the sway, I must needs remember that I have viewed the faces

*Considera-*
*tiones piæ.*

of some living persons, which upon the first sight
have made no greater an impression of sensuality
in my thoughts than if it had been no more but a
painted thing upon a sign post ; and yet the often
renewing of the same objects hath so much dis-
composed me in the end, that if grace had not
come to save me, my reason had been fooled, and
all had been utterly lost.

I have found by experience that my great
jealousy of my wordly reputation hath much disturbed my mind, endangered my soul, and hath
rather hindered than promoted what I aimed at.
For my honour can never receive a notable blemish
until I dishonour my Maker.   Worldly honour is
a shadow, that flies when you follow it, and follows
you when you fly it.

*Navigia
perforata.*          See the ' Intelligencer,' Monday, April 11, 1664,
p. 234—' Barbados, February 16.   In the latitude
2·50 south, 900 leagues eastward of this island,
a great fish struck the ship under the starboard
side, and passing under it touched the rudder and
threw the man from the helm ; and when she came
on the other side, heaved a great sea into the ship.
At her first stroke she ran her horn (or fin)

through the sheathing, a three-inch plank, through
the timber into the ceiling, and there brake it
short off. So that a piece of 12 inches long and
1½ c. weight was left in the hole. If the horn had
not been broken in the hole the vessel had been
lost ; for that stoppage notwithstanding, the water
came in so fast, that it kept a pump employed.
Since the ship came in here it hath been careened,
the piece taken out of the bulge, and the hole
stopped. The horn is like an elephant's tooth, but
more ponderous.'

Mr. Roger l'Estrange, in his letter to me on
occasion of this story (which I had touched upon
in some of my letters to him), writes thus : ' As to
the disproportionate (and indeed incredible) weight
of the fish bone, I delivered it as a wonder, but
not without an express direction of conformity to
the relation sent to his Royal Highness, however
mistaken.'

The weight assigned to the horn is of course an
absurd error. Nearly a century later we find the
following record of a similar event, taken from the
narrative of the crew of a ship from St. Eustatia to
Edinboro' : ' In our passage from the Main hither,
June 16, 1754, in lat. 15° long. 61°, we were struck
by a sword-fish, or sea-unicorn, on our starboard
bow, which ran his horn through our outside plank

(a timber of 10 inches thick) and ceiling into the
hold, broke his horn off, and left it in the hold 10
inches. We reckon that the horn went through
14½ inches of solid oak.' (Nichol's 'Literary Illus-
trations,' vol. iii. p. 800.)

Venefici Suf-
folcienses.

Mr. Howell's Letter 78, vol. ii. A.D. 1646, saith
'We have multitudes of witches among us, for in
Essex and Suffolk there were about 200 indited
within these two years, and about one half of them
executed: more I may say than ever this island
bred since the creation.' He saith that 'never a
cross is left to fright the devil away.'

Hibernicum
bellum et
cædes.

The cruelties of the Irish against the English
are in everybody's mouth, and set forth in printed
pageants sold in London. Some cruelties on the
contrary part are these that follow.

An English parson that lived in Ireland told
me that one of his own coat, born in Wirral in
Cheshire and beneficed in Ireland, killed with his
own hands one Sunday morning fifty-three of his
own parishioners, most or all of them (as I remember) women and children. This was told me at
Chester, A.D. 1644, in the hearing of Mr. Ralph
Bridoke, chaplain to the Earl of Derby.

Colonel Washington told of great cruelties committed by the soldiers against the Irish; among other things, that he saw one take an infant upon his pike and toss it up in the air.

Captain Robert Bramwel told me he was in danger of his life from his own party for covering a young gentlewoman with his cloak who had been stripped by them; they afterwards dashed out her brains.

One Captain Phillipson (as I take it), one of the English officers, told me that about 100 or 200 of unarmed Irish, that climbed up to the top of trees to avoid the soldiers, were all killed with shot from below, and that a child of two years old was barbarously (and oddly) murdered in the same place.

Archdeacon Pryce told me that Major Morice hanged a gentlewoman, only because she looked (as he was pleased to phrase it) like an Irish lady.

The 'Politician's Catechism' relateth briefly other sad particulars of this nature. Few of the populous country of Fingal left alive; all perished by fire and sword, being innocent people and having nothing Irish-like in them but the Catholic religion. The army killed man, woman, and child in the county of Wicklow. A gentlewoman, big

with child, was hanged on the arch of a bridge.
Mr. Comain, who never bare arms, was roasted
there alive by Captain Gines.   They murdered all
that came in their way from within two miles of
Dublin.   Mrs. Eustace of Cradockston in the
county of Kildare (sister to Sir William Talbot),
of 80 years of age, after she had entertained with
victuals, was murdered by the Protestant officers,
with another old gentlewoman and a girl of eight
years of age.   Mr. Cauley of Westmeath, showing
his protection, was killed with a shot, the protection being laid on his breast to try if it were proof.
Mr. Thomas Talbot, a great servitor in Queen
Elizabeth's wars in Ireland, aged 90 years, was
murdered tho' he had a protection.   From 700 to
800 women, children, and labourers were murdered
in one day in the King's land within seven miles
of Dublin.   And yet it may be a question whether
those great transplantations to Connaught and to
America exceed not all that hath been said.

Naves in-
gentiores.

Concerning the Royal Sovereign, see Howell's
' Ep. '  33.  sec.  6.   Her  length,  127  feet ;  her
greatest  breadth  within  the  planks,  46˙6 ;  her
depth from the breadth, 19 feet 4 inches.   The

charge of building, 80.000*l*. Her burthen, 1,636, which was the year in which she was built.

I saw this ship in 1660 lying in a dock at Chatham. I saw her dry to the keel and I did judge her to be about those very dimensions which Mr. Howell speaks of but not altogether so wide. This I can add, that her firm flat side in the port holes was 17 inches thick as near as may be.

A country song remembering the harmless mirth of Lancashire in peaceable times (1641). Tune, ' Roger o' Coverley :

> Robin and Ralph and Willy
> Took Susan and Ginnet and Cisly ;
> And Roger and Richard and Geordy
> Took Mary and Peggy and Margery ;
> And danced a hornpipe merrily :
> Tired out the bagpipe and fiddle
> With dancing the hornpipe and didle.

> But Gilbert and Thomas and Harry,
> Whose sweethearts were Nell, Nan and Marie,
> Took sides against Giles, James, and Richard,
> Whose wenches were Joan, Jane, and Bridget.
> The wager was for a wheat cake.
> They danced till their bones did ache
> That Gilbert and Nanny and Nellie
> Did sweat themselves into a jelly.

H H

The lads of Chowbent were there,
And had brought their dogs to the bear,
But they had no time to play,
They danced away the day ;
For thither then they had brought Knex
To play Chowbent hornpipe, that Nick's,
Tommy's and Geffrey's shoon
Were worn quite through with the tune.


The lads of Latham did dance
Their Lord Strange hornpipe, which once
Was held to have been the best,
And far to exceed all the rest.
But now they do hold it too sober,
And therefore will needs give it over.
They call on their piper then jovially,
' Play us brave Roger o' Coverley.'


The Meols men danced their Cop,
And about the may-pole did hop,
Till their shoes were so full of sand,
That they could no longer stand.
The Formby trotter supplied,
Who, though that his breeches were wide,
Yet would he ne'er give it o'er
Till the piper was ready to snore.


But Gilbert and Susan and Nanny,
With Tom and Dick, Cisly, and many,
Tripped and skipped full merrily,
The music now sounding out cheerily.

Dick booted, Nel flouted, he shouted
'Tak't thee James Pyper of Formby ;
Tak't thee, tak't thee, tak't thee,
Tak't thee James Pyper of Formby.'

At length it was time to go,
And Susan did hear the cock crow.
The maids might go make up their fires,
Or else be chid by their sires.
Next holyday, they'll ha' their fill
At Johnson's o' th' Talke of the hill,
Where Bell shall be brought to play.
Alack, how I long for that day !

The second part, to the tune of the 'Upstroke :'

That day it was past
On Tuesday last,
And you might have seen there,
If you had been there,
The lasses and louts
With smirkings and shouts.
Such did I ne'er hear on.
Good Lord, they would fear one.
For still they cried merrily,
'Hey for Crosby !
Hey Sefton ! hey Thornton !
Hey for Netherton ! '
Till hoarse they whopped.
Being weary they stopped.
Then cakes and prunes stewed
Were greedily chewed.
Of ale that was good
They poured down a flood.

And being got giddy,
Then stepped forth Neddy,
And swore by his fakins,
That he would go dance again ;
Aye, by the makins
Then hand in hand they went,
Cheerily, cheerily ;
Calling on their Bell,
Merrily, merrily.
All sport was forsaken
To see loose legs shaken.
But Rowland and Nelly,
With Susan and Billy,
Got all the glory.
That is in the story.
And those that are sager,
Say they won the wager ;
For whilst there was any day,
They would ne'er get away.

Mr. Blundell seems to have had some misgivings in leaving on record this lively sketch of the frolic and pastimes of his earlier days. In the margin he has written ' Ne reminiscaris, Domine, delicta juventutis meæ—Remember not, O Lord, the sins of my youth.' We gather from the context, that he is pourtraying some of the festivities connected with the rearing of the May-pole. By King Charles' warrant, October 18, 1633, it was enacted that ' for his good people's lawful recreation, after the end of Divine Service, his good people be not disturbed, letted, or discouraged from any lawful recreation : such as dancing, either men or women ; archery for men, leaping, vaulting, or any other such harmless

recreations ; nor from having of May Games, Whitson ales, and Morris dances, and the setting up of
May-poles, and other sports therewith used,' &c. In
1644, May-poles, described as a heathenish vanity,
were ordered by the Commonwealth to be destroyed
throughout the Kingdom. After the restoration they
were again permitted to be erected, and the custom
held its ground almost to our own time. Within
the last half century, May-poles and the festivities
connected with them have gradually become things
of the past ; but memorials of them, and traditions
of their sites, are still abundant. The gathering
round the May-pole of Crosby must have been very
large, as it comprised the youth not only of the
neighbouring villages, Formby, Sefton, Netherton,
and Thornton, but also of the more remote ones,
Meols and Lathom. The first ceremony was decking the pole with flowers, and this was done by the
fair hands of the village maidens. To this custom
Herrick alludes ; for the May-pole figures in those
loose and flowing numbers with which at this very
period he was beguiling the tedium of his solitary
life at Dean Prior :

> ' The May-pole is up
> Now give me the cup ;
> I'll drink to the garlands around it ;
> But first unto those
> Whose hands did compose
> The glory of flowers that crowned it.'

Then the rearing took place ; and the pole was
fixed in its position amidst the tumultuous cheers of
the assembled crowd. A general dance round the
newly-erected pole followed, and in this everybody

took part, joining hand to hand.  At Crosby, the
squire himself, who, though already married, was
then but twenty-one, would certainly be present to
witness, if not to participate in the dance.

'The lords of castles, mannors, townes and towers,
    Rejoic'd when they beheld the farmers flourish ;
And would come down unto the summer bowers,
    To see the country-gallants dance the Morrice.'
                        (Pasquil's ' Palinodia,' 1634.)

Mr. Blundell has recorded his love of dancing, but
the fatal accident he met with in the eventful year
which followed these festivities, put an end to his
capacity for such amusements.  The dancing on
these occasions was kept up with great spirit, assisted
by the piper's melody.  In those days almost every
township had its piper or fiddler, for the two instruments in vogue were the bagpipes and fiddle.
Some of these pipers were no mean proficients on
their instruments.  Thomas Knex, of Chowbent,
was a noted piper, and he must have received a
special invitation to join this gathering.  The lads
of Chowbent, which is thirty miles from Crosby,
would hardly have made so long a journey unless
they had come in the train of their celebrated
player.  The Cavalier's grandson, Nicholas Blundell,
has the following entry in his diary, regarding Anderton, the piper :—

'1707, January 31.—I sold my horse Buck to
William Anderton for one day's playing of the pipes
per annum, as long as he lives in Lancashire, and
for 25*s.* to be paid by parcels as he can get it ; if
the horse prove ill, I promise to bate him 5*s.*'

The Chowbent lads had brought their dogs to

the bear, as the barbarous sport of bear-baiting usually formed part of the May-pole festivities. There was generally a bear-garden in each township ; that at Lydiate was let in 1682 at 3*l.* per annum. The bears were chiefly itinerant, and there must have been a large supply for the whole of England. To this pastime we may suppose that the lads from Chowbent were specially addicted ; for we have been accustomed to associate with that spot ideas and customs not the most refined. But it is fair to remind our readers that Chowbent has recently undergone the purification of railway official baptism, and has begun a new life in the character of mild-mannered Atherton.

The dancers contended for prizes, but these were of a Spartan simplicity of character, 'the prize it was a wheat-cake.' The winners were apparently those who could remain longest upon their legs, and the lusty lads and country lasses must have taxed the patience of the spectators, to say nothing of the pipers, by their powers of endurance. Cakes, stewed prunes, and ale was the fare provided, and no doubt much of the last was consumed, but Mr. Blundell does not speak of any excess. Prunes were then largely imported into Liverpool and much used in the country districts around it. Mr. Nicholas Blundell, the diarist, records that Mr. Houghton, a merchant of Liverpool, told him that he had once imported eight casks of prunes, from which he expected no small profit. He warehoused them carefully, but on examining them a few months later, he found to his dismay that the rats had got into the casks, and had eaten every kernel out of the prunes. Talk-on-t'hill (Tulketh Hill), formerly outside Preston, is now absorbed in that town. This was the scene of the second festive gathering commemorated by Mr. Blundell in another metre—the whole forming an amusing and spirited description of May-pole festivities in the year of Grace 1641.

Sabbath.   The Scots are severe in keeping the Sunday holyday. They do not permit a barber or a bottle of wine to come into a gentleman's lodging through the streets. My son William tells me that he heard Mr. Alexander Rigby (who was newly come thence to Haigh in November 1669), relate this following story. The Earl of Athole's brother had his wine taken by the guards, who drank it off as it was coming through the streets to his chamber. Whereupon he sent a bottle partly filled with poison and partly with sack, which the guards took and drank, and were sundry of them grievously sick, whereof one lay in great danger of death when the said Mr. Rigby (who was then a companion of the said Earl's brother, when the deed was done), came out of the kingdom.

The peasants about Rome do come on Sundays to hear Mass in the city, from whence after noon they carry their weekly bread home which they do buy in the city. This was told me by Mr.

Edward Anderton, March 1669-70. He told me further that workmen did publicly expose themselves there on a Sunday in the streets or market, where it is the custom to hire them for the following week.

Nine persons may enter at a door or sit at a table 362,700 times, and each of those times with a different precedence. I mean in such sort as that all of them shall never be twice in the same order, which may be well expressed by these nine figures, 1 2 3 4 5 6 7 8 9, which may be varied 362,700 times. *Plura quam putares.*

Twelve (e.g. the twelve bells in Bow Church, which I have seen and counted) may be varied with different changes 478,764,000 times.

Consider the life of some virtuous poor souls— Bridget Stock, for example. She is disabled to work, hath nothing whereby to subsist, being neither a beggar from door to door, nor relieved by a tax on the parish. Some little work she can do to earn perhaps a penny a day, and that but sometimes. A raging sore leg hath long tormented her, the bone is almost bare for a long way. She *Eleemosynæ.*

I I

sells her best clothes to buy salve for this, and alas! to little purpose. Now, in the winter, she keeps no other fire (or at the most exceeding little), but to melt her salve. Her windy, cold house is very small and uncomfortable, and she lives in a poor town, where the relief they bring her is very scant. She is born of good friends, is fair and young, and a virtuous patient soul. The sixth part of one extravagant madam's useless ribbons would relieve twenty such maids as these, and yet one of these maids is worth 10,000 of those madams.

*Vi luæ.* It was the saying of a widower who had children, when he was asked why he did not marry again, ' Liberorum causâ duxeram uxorem ; liberorum causâ rursus non duxi.' Colloquium senile. 240. [I married a wife for the sake of children ; for the sake of my children I have not married again].

*Observationes politicæ.* A man must be twenty or thirty years in raising a fortune ; the business is hardly done till he be growing up to sixty; when he is an old man he begins to build a fine house, and just when he finishes it, he drops away.

1681.—After my master, W. B. Esq., had been Physic and doctor's bill. long ill of a violent cold, Dr. Worthington came first unto him on January 8. He staid two nights and received for his pains 1*l.* 10*s.* He brought along with him, and left with my master, a kind of syrup or consistence in a small earthen pot ; this he called Lohoch. He brought also ten pills, with a bottle of spirits somewhat bigger than one's thumb, and a paper of lozenges, with French barley and several ingredients for the making the water thereof. On the 11th day he sent a glister, with a large pint bottle of a cordial julep, and a small bottle of syrups to be sucked up with a liquorice stick, also some small quantity of sal-prunella. On the 21st day he sent by way of Liverpoole a bottle containing, as we guess, five or six ounces of syrups, also another bottle less by more than half than the former, containing the oil of sweet almonds, together with ten pills. His letter of instructions, which came then, mentions some spirits and sugared oil which were not delivered. The doctor was with my master the second time on January 17, and received for his pains 15*s.* This is writ by me Walter Thelwall, by my master's order. Note, that the spirits and sugared oil were brought to my master by Mr. Thomas Worthington on January 24, and were both of them to be taken together mixed with barley water and other beverage.

The elder Lady Bradshaigh sent my master a bottle containing, as we guess, about one ounce of balsam, which in her letter she calls (if we read it aright) balsam of sulphur. Her ladyship there saith that it is an approved cure for a cough ; that she had it from Sir Peter Brooks that it had cured him of a most violent cough, and that the Lady Ossory had sent it to him. That it must be taken morning and night, three or four drops naked and alone in a spoon, that it must be a little warmed before it will drop at all, by reason it is thick and clammy.

### Copy of Dr. Worthington's Bill.

#### For Mrs Blundell, sen.

|  | £ | s. | d. |
|---|---|---|---|
| 1681, Oct. 24—Spirits . . . . | o | 4 | 6 |
| An ointment . . . | o | 1 | 4 |

#### For Mr. Blundell, sen.

|  | £ | s. | d. |
|---|---|---|---|
| 1681, Jan. 8—Spirits . . . . | o | 4 | 6 |
| Ten pills . . . | o | 2 | o |

|  | £ | s. | d. |
|---|---|---|---|
| A Lohoch . . . | 0 | 2 | 0 |
| Lozenges . . . | 0 | 4 | 0 |
| Jujubes and sebertines . | 0 | 0 | 8 |
| French barley . . | 0 | 1 | 0 |
| Ingredients . . . | 0 | 1 | 6 |
| Syrups . . . . | 0 | 3 | 0 |
| A cordial julep . . | 0 | 10 | 6 |
| A glister . . . | 0 | 2 | 6 |
| 1681, Jan. 11—Syrups . . . . | 0 | 3 | 0 |
| White powder . . | 0 | 0 | 4 |
| Five pills . . . | 0 | 1 | 3 |
| The oiled sugar . . | 0 | 7 | 0 |
| Syrups . . . | 0 | 5 | 6 |
| Oil of sweet almonds . | 0 | 1 | 8 |
| Spirits of ptisanne . . | 0 | 7 | 6 |
| For a messenger . . | 0 | 1 | 6 |
|  | £3 | 5 | 3 |

My master's opinion of these several things in particular is here to be inserted for farther use, viz., That the *spirits* first named, of which twenty-six drops were put into one small cup of barley water and beer or into barley water alone, had no apparent effect, although he doth not much doubt

but the secret effect might be good.    That the like
might be said of the *pills* mentioned in two places;
although it seemed that they did somewhat as-
suage his cough, which was extremely violent.
The *Lohoch*, a liquor like a syrup, did apparently
bring up phlegm, and was well liked.   The *lozenges*
were pleasant, and did sometimes stop the cough.
*Barley water* with the ingredients was cooling and
pleasant.    Syrups, twice mentioned, although of
much different prices, seemed to be the same.
They seemed to stop the cough, and bring up
phlegm.   The *cordial julep*, of which there was a
large pint bottle, was pleasant, but the effect not
apparent.    The *glister* extraordinarily effective
and good.   *White powder*, supposed to be sal-
prunella, assuaged thirst.   The *oiled sugar* with the
*spirits of ptisanne*, besides the extreme dearness,
were almost wholly useless in regard that the
patient, being much on the mending hand when
they were sent unto him, drunk little barley water,
and these were only to be infused in that beverage.
He sent back to the doctor about seven-eighths of
the oiled sugar, and yet he paid for the whole.
The *oil of sweet almonds*, of which seven or eight
drops were taken in a bolus of white sugar candy,

frequently helped the breast, made very sore by coughing.

> Dr. Thomas Worthington lived at Wigan, and some mention of him occurs in ' Lydiate Hall and its Associations,' where it is recorded (page 125) that he was obliged to sell his goods and fly from that town at the time of the ferment which followed the pretended discoveries of Titus Oates. As he is found attending Mr. Blundell in 1681, he must have soon returned, and his death is mentioned by Mr. Nicholas Blundell as having occurred on November 27, 1701. He reached the age of 83, and his son Francis, called by Mr. Nicholas Blundell, Dr. Fanny Worthington, continued the practice of medicine in Wigan, and is frequently mentioned both in the Tyldesley and Blundell Diaries.

September 12, 1666.—I did engage with my cousin Henry Blundell of Ince Blundell, Esq., to join 40*l.* with him as an adventure to the Barbadoes in the good ship called the ' Antelope ' of Liverpoole, and he undertook at the same time to Dr. Richmond to become a merchant for that voyage for one-fourth part of the said ship to Barbadoes and back to Liverpoole, for which he is to pay 3*l.* per ton thither and 6*l.* back. Dr. Richmond said that 80*l.* would be sufficient for him and me to venture for the fourth part of the said ship.

Traffique at sea

September 15.—I delivered 40*l.* to my son to bring for that purpose to my cozen Blundell or to John Laithwaite (Mr. H. Blundell's steward).

October 11.—I received from my sister Winefrid 5*l.* as one-eighth part of my adventure abovesaid, and she is for that to have one-eighth part of my profit, paying for the tonnage, according as I do myself, over and above this 5*l.*

The 'Antelope' went from Leverpoole, Monday, September 15, towards Barbadoes, 1666.

1667, August 19.—The 'Antelope' returned to Leverpoole from the Barbadoes.

1667, November 1.—I received upon account 83*l.* 6*s.*, and the next day 2*s.* 6*d.* more from my cozen Blundell. And there yet remains to be accounted for one butt of sugar, besides 1,300 lbs. weight of sugar left at Barbadoes.

1671, July 7.—This day I call to mind that I did receive betwixt 3*l.* and 4*l.* more than is mentioned above, viz., for the odd parcel of sugar late mentioned, and I cleared all with my sister.

Observationes politicæ.

Our excess and curiosity in victuals, furniture and apparell, &c., are often destructive to ourselves and to the Commonwealth. What wonders were wrought by the Spartans and other ancient nations, who avoided all excess of this kind. There is one that observeth (and seemeth in a sort of demonstrate), what a vast advantage would arise to this nation if all would observe abstinence from flesh on those days on which the Catholic Church commandeth it. And it is not to be doubted but the money which would yearly be saved (if all the nation would agree to regard no other thing but warmness and other useful conveniences in their habits), might keep in continual pay a considerable army. And this besides providing competently for the necessities of such as otherwise would be like to perish, because their superfluous handicrafts would now be unuseful.

King James and King Charles I. proclaimed a licence to the people to use sundry recreations upon Sundays, and particularly the sport of dancing after evening prayer. In April 1660, I saw the Dukes of York and Gloucester, with their sister the Princess of Orange, play a long time at ninepins upon a Sunday, whilst the King their brother looked on. It was at Breda. Sabbatum.

K K

*Amicus et amicitia.*

Mr. Langhorne, in his letter to me of September 5, 1668, speaking of his long silence, saith, 'Friendship is a marriage of two affections, and if either party fail sometimes in their duty (as of late I have done), yet it is no real disobligation, so far as to justify the other in a failure of what is just in him to practise.'

*Tenants book.*

I do hereby strictly charge and conjure my heir, and so far as lawfully I may (who have all my estate now in fee simple) I do obleege him hereby in strict justice, that (notwithstanding what he may find written in any book of mine) he do regard the heir of John Howard according as he regardeth or ought to regard his ancient tenants. And I do farther desire my heir to show sometimes unto the said John and his children some marks of particular favour, which may be known to be chiefly done in memory and gratitude for the long and faithful service of his uncle Edward Denton, performed to my grandfather and myself. Witness of what I have here required and desired —my hand—William Blundell, June 15, 1663.

*Plumbum.*

The pits where lead is digged, in Derbyshire, are

called grooves. I was informed by many there, that these pits are extremely narrow, viz., not one yard square, and yet forty fathom deep, and some of them more. The price of lead at the mill (as Wm. Harrison, who deals much therein, told me, 1668) is now at 10*l.* 10*s.* a fodder, which is very cheap. About the year 1663 it was more than 15*l.* A fodder is eight-horse load (as he saith), each load being 21 stone and a half, of 15 to the stone, each pound being 18 ounces. This seems to be a great horse load, but the account is very confused. I was told as for certain, that anybody might get lead anywhere in another man's ground where the same is known to be, allowing the owner of the land a thirteenth part. This is in the Peak of Derbyshire.

On May 1, 1673, Sir Thomas Clifton made a relation to me at Scarisbrick to this effect, viz., 'On Monday se'night my wife, told me that she had dreamed that herself and her cousin Scarisbrick and his brother Thomas were all of them laid out in white as if they were dead.' Sir Thomas did then express in many words, what trouble of mind he had to hear so speedily after

The Lady Clifton, her dream.

the death of my cousin Thomas Scarisbrick, which happened on April 23 (but two days after we had heard of my lady's dream), and then again to hear of my cousin Scarisbrick's death, which happened on the 29th of the same, at whose burial on May 1, he made this relation to me.

All this above I wrote on May 2, 1673, and this I shall add, that my cousin Scarisbrick was in health when my Lady told that dream : and I think it is true that my Lady did not then know anything of my cousin Thomas his sickness, which had been but a day or two. If my Lady (who I think is now in health) die within a short time, I shall not doubt but the matter was revealed unto her by a special favour from God ; otherwise I shall not well know how to interpret the dream or rely on the relation.

The recorded pedigrees of the Clifton family do not give the date of Lady Clifton's death, but it is highly probable that if it had taken place within a short time, Mr. Blundell would have added a note to this effect. She was Bridget, daughter of Sir Edward Hussey, Knt. of Honington, co. Lincoln, and second wife to Sir Thomas, who had been created Bart., 1660. Dying in 1694 without male issue, the title expired while the estates descended to his nephew. Thomas Scarisbrick, Priest, S.J., had resided with the Cliftons at Lytham, and seems to have been on a visit to Scarisbrick when he caught a fever of which both he and his elder brother died. James Scarisbrick, of Scarisbrick, Esq., had married Frances fifth daughter of Robert Blundell, of Ince Blundell, Esq., by whom he left a young family. She survived her husband 47 years.

In June 1695 I caused my man, Walter Thel- Stadium Crosbiense. wall, with the help of another person, to measure the Crosby course exactly with a chain, and this was the result, each rood being 24 feet :

| | Roods. | yds. |
|---|---|---|
| From the chair or starting place to the sea-post . . . . . . | 82 | 4 |
| From the sea-post to the left-hand post | 81 | 0 |
| From the left-hand post to the plat . | 122 | 0 |
| From the plat to the post on the More-house marsh . . . . . | 118 | 0 |
| | 403 | 4 |

The total, ridden twice over to make the course complete, amounts to 807 roods.

That which followeth is a copy of my letter to Tenant-right. Mr. Henry Howard (*alias* Ireland), and his answer

thereunto was written on the back of my said
letter :—

To Mr. Henry Howard at Chester, October 7,
1654.—I beseech you, do me the great favour to
give me your opinion in the cases of conscience
following :

1. What doth the claim of the heir of a deceased tenant (commonly called tenant right)
amount to in Lancashire after his father's lease is
expired ?  If you be not acquainted with the
ground of their claim, I will give it you as best I
can.  The landlords in that county have generally
admitted the heirs of former tenants not only
before another, but at a much lower rate than any
other ; so that where a stranger will pay ten years'
value at the least for a lease of three lives, the heir
of the former tenant shall have the same for six
years' value.  Very good landlords will take but
the half from the heir that a stranger will give him ;
some will take less than the one half.  There are
some again (but not many) that turn them quite off
without any regard to the claim.  These last are
railed upon and cursed, and many of the former
cannot 'scape it.  We know no law to cause these
favours, nor anything but the custom of our

country, to use our tenants kindly, which is variable according to the landlords' humour, affection, &c.

2. In case the landlord be bound in conscience to bate something considerable to the late tenant's heir, of that which a stranger will give, and a stranger bids 100*l.* fine, and the lord will let a deserving tenant take it for 50*l.*, and yet make a tenant in the like case that he thinks undeserving to pay 60*l.* or 65*l.*, or else go without it, is there any injury in that? By *undeserving* I understand all great misdemeanours, or notable disrespect to his landlord for which the landlord would punish him.

3. The landlord supposeth that when a stranger will give 100*l.* he may safely take 60*l.* of the heirs to preceding tenants. But yet he resolveth to take but 50*l.* or less of all such tenants as shall please him, and of those that shall displease him to take 60*l.* Is not the supposition true, and the resolution of the landlord lawful, provided he do it for example's sake and not for revenge?

A resolution of the cases expressed.

1. I say that by the laws of England, as they have been expounded by divers judges in open

court, there is no tenant-right at all remaining when their leases are fully expired. The reason and ground for this is, because the land being the lord's the tenant can claim no more right than that the lord of the land did grant by the bargain expressed in his lease ; therefore, when his lease is fully expired, the former bargain is wholly ended, and consequently there remains no tenant-right at all.

2. I say in answer to the first case, that there is a probable opinion commonly received by the best divines in England, that what is law betwixt party and party as concerning the right of private persons without any penalty for religion or delinquency, is also good and lawful in conscience. Wherefore, as by the laws of England there is no tenant-right at all when the lease is fully expired, so by this probable opinion there is no obligation of conscience for the landlord to give or grant anything for tenant-right after the tenant's lease is fully expired.

3. I answer concerning the same first case, that the custom of the country begets no tenant-right, nor brings any obligation at all upon the landlord to give, grant, or allow anything at all for it. The

reason for this is, that the most that can be said for the custom is, that there has been formerly and peradventure there may still remain an opinion amongst many, that there is some such tenant-right brought in by custom, and, to grant unto these as much as can be required, that this their opinion should be allowed for probable and still in practice amongst many. Yet, notwithstanding, should all this be granted, being as much as any can say for that side, it is without all doubt most certain that the opposite opinion that denies any such tenant-right brought in by custom is at the least probable, as hath been sufficiently proved. Wherefore it is lawful not only by the laws of England, but also in conscience, for any landlord to choose and follow whichever opinion he shall like the best. For it is a certain principle amongst divines, that in all cases where there are two opposite opinions and both probable, it is lawful in conscience for any one in particular to follow which opinion he will, and if any therefore shall curse or clamour against him, it is for no fault he has committed, but a bad effect of their own malicious mind.

Now, to come to the second case. First, I say in that opinion of such as will hold landlord bound in conscience to bate something considerable to the late tenant's heir of that which a stranger will give, it is no wrong or injury at all to make an undeserving tenant to pay 60*l.* or 65*l.* or to go without it, as the second case relates. For the opinion that makes for tenant-right brought in by custom does not prescribe in particular what the landlord is bound to do, but leaves landlords to their own discretion, which teacheth more is in reason fitting to be done for one well deserving or that has not given any cause of offence, than for any undeserving man such as your case describes. Secondly, I say to this second case, that by the other opinion which admits no tenant-right after the lease is fully expired, that of an undeserving tenant you may take what you will more than you would of another, so you do not exceed the just price that strangers would give for it, and that you do not do it out of any anger or ill will towards him, but for any good motives of virtue, to teach him and others by example how to perform their duty.

By this that hath been already said, you may gather a full answer to all the rest you have writ. For seeing there is a probable opinion that admits of no tenant-right at all after the lease is fully

expired, whatsoever you shall bate to any tenant
of that a stranger would give, is a favour which
you may show more or less as you shall see cause
for it.—(Hen. Ho., October 11, 1654.)

It is difficult to identify this Henry Howard *alias*
Ireland. Sir Thomas Haggerston, second Bart. of
Haggerston, Northumberland, had two sons, Henry
and John, who became Jesuits and were known by
the *alias* of Howard, their mother being Margaret,
daughter of Sir Francis Howard of Corby. These,
however, belonged to the next generation, and the
Henry Haggerston of the earlier period, a brother-in-
law of Mr. Blundell's, was a married layman who
had borne some part in the Civil War on behalf of
the King. Of the Ireland family of Lydiate, Alexander, born 1604, became a priest and entered the
Society of Jesus in 1640. In 1632 a younger
brother, Thomas, in answer to interrogatories on entering the English College, Rome, declares that he
has two brothers, priests, one a secular (Alexander),
and the other a Jesuit, but gives no names. This
may possibly be the missing brother, but it is more
likely, from Mr. Blundell's usual mode of writing,
that the real name of the casuist was Howard.

In solving the question, prominence is given to
the doctrine of probabilism, which was then in great
repute. Concina, in his ' Della Storia del Proba-
bilismo' (Lucca, 1743, vol. i. p. 18), says that Barto.
Medina, a Dominican, first broached this doctrine,
A.D. 1577, in a work on the Summa of St. Thomas.
It did not attract much attention till 1620, when a
book of P. Milhard advocating it was prohibited by

the Sorbonne.   This gave rise to wider discussions,
and these opinions, growing into favour, were taken
up in the Jesuit schools.  Sanchez, Layman, Garasse,
and especially Diana, who is called the 'Lamp of
Probabilism,' became the chief exponents of this
doctrine.  Mr. Blundell's correspondent, in his reply,
seems to have regarded more the requirements of
justice than those of custom or charity.  He has
perhaps not allowed sufficient weight to obligations
arising from a custom then clearly established by
long and universal usage.  It has been already remarked that the practice of granting leases for three
lives has of late years been generally abandoned.
Whatever Mr. Blundell may have thought of his
correspondent's opinion, he continued to the end
of his life to follow his accustomed plan of favouring
old tenants by requiring from them only a six or
seven years' fine, while exacting from a stranger
one of ten or twelve years.  At the same time he
would doubtless use his liberty in the extreme case
of very undeserving tenants.

*Atheos.*

Father Warner, the Provincial of the English
Jesuits, told me in 1681 of a late professed Atheist,
who was (as I take it) well known to him, that
wished he had lost an arm on condition that he
could have firm Christian faith.

*Retorquia
acute.*

The merry tale told by Jo. Molineux of the
drunken frolics betwixt the Lord Goring and Admiral Opdam.  Opdam having been pressed to

sacrifice some garments of better value than the rest of the drinkers had, to the health of the King, took the like advantage of Goring, and caused him to burn a cloth of gold doublet on the like occasion. Which affront was retorted on Opdam, when Goring caused a fœtid tooth to be plucked out of his own head, to the honour of the party they drank to, and Opdam (for shame) was constrained to second the frolic with a sound tooth.

George Lord Goring, the Royalist general, possessed undoubted courage, but his life was vicious. Having gained his pardon and lost his estate, he retired in the time of the interregnum to the little Court of Charles II., and his manners were perfectly adapted to it when it rose to the height of frolic and debauchery (Granger's ' Biography '). He was created Earl of Norwich in 1645, having married Lady Ann Denney, sister and ultimately co-heir of her brother Edward, who had received that Earldom in 1626, and had died without issue. He died suddenly in 1662. No doubt the meetings with Admiral Opdam would take place at the King's Court abroad. This Dutch Admiral had the reputation of being a skilful and brave commander. He met with his death in the famous naval engagement of June 1, 1665, which covered with laurels the unfortunate James II., then Admiral of the English fleet. It is said that Opdam was forced by the peremptory orders of his Government to give battle, although much against his own judgment. Sir Charles Sedley is elsewhere described as the hero of the above story.

Commoda
reipublicæ
optanda.

To prevent quarrels and jostles in the streets, it were not amiss that all that have the wall on their right hand might go next to the wall. This would cause almost all persons to pass one way, i.e. all on one side of the street to go one way and the rest another way. It is the custom in Italy (especially where enemies do meet) to play for the precedence at a game, which in Latin is called '*micare digitis.*'

It were good that the miscarriage of a business should not be a bettering of the reward of him that miscarries it. Why should the nurses of sick persons (especially in London) have all that they find upon them when they die ? Doth it not make them to desire they may die ? Lawyers and their clerks get the more money if they make the deeds superfluously long ; the inconvenience of which is unspeakable in two respects.

I found once the tails of my cattle cut almost to the rump. The cowman did this, who had the hair for a fee.

Tithes and
church dues.

We pay the tithe of corn in kind. Hay we compound for. In 1662 I paid for the tithe hay of my demesne at Crosby, 17s. In 1663, 16s.

For many years together during the Usurpation, I paid 13*s.* and 13*s.* 4*d.* But about the year 1639, we paid little less than 40*s.* for the Hall and the Town. Wool is paid in kind. For hemp, 1*s.* the bushel seeding ; for flax, 1*s.* ditto. If it do appear that we have ten calves, of which by rearing, selling, or killing, we have had any profit, we must pay for tithe 20*s.* If we have seven calves or upwards, we pay as much as for ten calves, only we have to receive back for every calf short of ten 1*s.* For five calves we pay 10*s.*, and for fewer 1*s.* for each calf.

I paid, 1664, for one lamb, 2*s.* 6*d.* ; for hay, 16*s.* ; for half a calf, 10*s.* But that year I had more than twelve kine, and commonly, when I had ten or twelve kine, I came off with half a calf. For christening and churching, 4*d.* ; for weddings published in the church, 1*s.* 8*d.*, and for their marriage ; for marrying by the parson with a licence and not asked in the church, 6*s.*

Smoke, 1*d.* Garden, ½*d.* Windmill, 1*s.* For eggs at Easter, twelve eggs are paid or 2*d.* ; 1*d.* for the master, as much for the dame, and but one halfpenny for each other person at all. Receiving at Easter : clerk's wages, 1*d.* ; one colt, 1*d.* Leys for the repairs of the church, everybody in the town pays 2*d.*

The Lord Gerard of Brandon told me in the hearing of my nephew Selby, Hy. Banister and others, May 18, 1663, that the late King had 900 servants, whereof no more than twenty-seven engaged with him in the late war. He said there were very few lawyers that adhered to the King, and spoke ill as to the same thing of the nobility in general that were made before the war. He said at the same time, that the King's cause was truly and constantly maintained by the English gentry.

Thomas Selby, Esq., of Biddlestone, Northumberland, owed much to the care and good counsel of his uncle. He met with an early death on December 6, 1666. Mr. Henry Banister, of Bank, came to a melancholy end, being slain at the races at Delamere (Sir Philip Egerton's) in April 1665. His murderer Colket, or Colcoth, was hanged at Chester for the crime. A diary of Roger Low, mercer, of Ashton-in-Makerfield, has this entry :

'1665, April 3.—Mr. Banister de Banke came through Ashton, being slain at the forest of Delamere, being accompanied by a store of gentry.' He was son of Henry Banister of Bank, Esq. (ob. 1641), married to Dorothy, daughter of Roger Nowell of Read, who survived him. They had no children.

(Local Gleanings, vol. i.) Mr. Blundell says in a letter to Lawrence Ireland that it was a drunken quarrel.

August 22, 1664.—At the Swan, in the Strand, *Statura hominum.* near Charing Cross, I saw (for 6*d.*) John Dodes, as I understood him, a Hollander, born at Schonhaven. All I could do, standing flat on my heels, was to reach with the point of my long finger to the very top or middle part of his head. His shoes were full three inches, as I take it, high on the heel. I could not reach with my head to his armpit by a full handfull. His wife was there, a woman of a middle or rather of a mean stature. He had had two children, both of whom were dead. I asked him for one Gerrard, his neighbour, whom I had heard, as I told him, to be higher than himself. He did not deny it, but said that the man was crook-shouldered or deformed. This John said he was himself twenty-eight years old, and that he was grown the breadth of his thumb since the age of twenty-seven. He was a handsome straight man in appearance, but he wore an Indian gown. He said he had been in Turkey (I saw him in a turban), and that he had been in Paris, where he received at the first half-a-crown of all that saw him, and that he took less and less.

Leo.

The weekly news-book called the 'Intelligencer,' printed Monday, July 25, 1664, tells us of an overgrown elephant sent by the Persian to the Great Turk, and how a lion was turned to him, which after they had gazed awhile did assail the elephant. The elephant did forthwith throw him up with his proboscis, with the bruise of which the lion being astonished was trodden or crushed to death by the said elephant. This is confirmed by many who say that the lion is dead.

Justitia
civilis.

An excessive multitude of laws is the destruction of justice. When they can hardly all be read by one man, they are not possible to be remembered or comprehended. And if rigid penal laws do abound in a great measure, they settle an arbitrary power : for whereas the rigour is too great to be put into frequent execution, it must necessarily come to this, that the magistrate must punish or release offenders according to his own pleasure. Quære, whether for the very same reason a multitude of pious laws and universal customs in the Church (I mean such as are painful or costly) do not, after some time, undoubtedly occasion the like effect ; the prelates being forced either to dispense, or connive at the breaking of the same. And hereby may probably have risen the slender regard which is given in many places to holy-days and fasting-days.

I have thought sometimes that it might have good success, if one should collect the whole proceedings, charges, writings, and troubles, which have belonged to some particular suits of small concernment. Then to publish in print a relation of the same with the hard terms of the law mentioned in the margin, not forgetting the abbreviations, the Latin, the French, and the strange hands. This may be useful to deter people from suits, and to induce them to submit to arbitration. The best examples for that purpose may be taken out of our Chanceryes, where all is done upon record ; and I would have the bill printed with the answer thereunto, as likewise the reply and rejoinder, and let it be mentioned what sheets they contained.

Articles for Races at Crosby, drawn up by W. B. at the request of Hon. W. Molyneux, to be run on 1st Monday in August 1682, and yearly afterwards :— *Stadium Crosbiense.*

1. It is articled and agreed upon, that a piece of silver plate, or plate consisting of sundry pieces of silver, shall be then exposed upon the stoop,

commonly called the chair, where the horse course
on Crosby Marsh doth usually begin and end, and
that the said plate shall be given to such horse,
mare or gelding, as by the observance of these
articles shall win the same.

2. Horse to be brought to the ground ten days
before the race, aired and trained there, housed and
fed within a mile and a half of the course. Name
of horse and person who intends to put him in to
be given two days before the horse comes to the
ground, to a qualified person or subscriber of 20s.

3. Every person bringing a horse to deposit 40s.
as a stake eight days before the race, which stake
or stakes either to be given to a second horse, or
held for another race next year, as the subscribers
may judge, 40s. subscribers to the plate exempted.
No subscriber to bring more than one horse.

4. Horses to be drawn out on the race-day at
two p.m., and weigh with rider and accoutrements
ten stone.

5. And whereas the limits of the said course,
by reason of long discontinuance, are unknown to
many persons, every rider in the race shall leave
the three first stoops, which stand upon the marsh
belonging to Great Crosby and next to the town

so called, all of them on his right hand, but the fourth and last stoop standing on the said marsh to be left on the left hand of the rider, at whose choice it shall be to leave the distance post and the post or chair, at the end, either on the one hand or the other.

6. That the horse which shall first end the first course or heat by returning back to the starting post, and by carrying his rider thither with his full weight or within a pound thereof, before any horse be come back to the distance post which stands upon the same ground, about twelve score yards from the end, shall win the plate. But if no such thing happen, a second heat to be run at the end of half an hour with horses not distanced. Again, after another half-hour, a third heat if necessary.

7. In case the plate be not gained in three heats, the horse coming in first in two, and within the distance in the one he loses, shall have the plate. If two different horses win the first and second, the winner of third shall take it.

8. Riders not submitting to the rules to be excluded from winning. A cloth or flag to be placed at the top of the ending post, to be let fall immediately the first horse comes to the end.

9. If only one horse come, he must take the plate after galloping over the course. Riders and horses to be weighed afresh after each heat, and before he enter the scales, a flagon of beer to be given to each rider if he require it.

10. Three gentlemen to be chosen by the majority of subscribers, for umpires in case of dispute.

The foregoing rules have been somewhat condensed, but they contain all essential particulars. There is frequent mention of Crosby races, from 1702 to 1728, in the Diary of Nicholas Blundell, Esq.

*Palatia nobi-liora.*

Chatsworth in Derbyshire, within the Peak, is the Earl of Devonshire's house, most stately and noble. I take the pile to be about 100 yards square on the outside. It is built about a court. My lord told me that it cost in building 80,000*l.*, and that the less of his two houses at Hardwick cost 30,000*l.* Chatsworth was built about the year 1573, and the little house abovesaid about 1597, both of them, and also Oldcotes (which was sold by his lordship to the Earl of Kingston), were built by Elizabeth, Countess of Shrewsbury.

The great chamber at the less house at Hardwick is 26 of my long paces in length, and 12 wide. That and the gallery (which is, as my lord saith, accounted to be 60 yards long, though he thinks it is but 57) are, as my lord saith, 30 feet high. But the gallery seemed to me to want about a large foot (as I judged by the four heights of the windows) of 30 feet in height, and I take the hall to be as high as the gallery. The gallery is over the hall, which makes a most stately high pile, exceedingly full of windows.

The new gallery at the Duke of Newcastle's house, called Bolsover, is in length (as his Grace's architect told me) 72 yards, 22½ feet wide, and about the same height. In the great chamber there is almost 29 of my large paces long, and almost 12 wide, and half a foot higher than the gallery.

My Lord of Devonshire told me Sir Benjamin Rydicar did write these verses on Chatsworth :—

> A woman thus composed much love would win,
> Hard of access, fair without, fair within.

But these verses or rhymes, written in large gold letters over the dining-room chimney, I am sure are bald ones :—

> Truly to serve in sight, duly by day or night,
> My Prince with all my might, such is my nature right.

Many other worse rhymes, and most ridiculously
spelt, are written there in large gold letters.    In
the drawing chamber at Hardwick, where a stag
(or two stags) supports a coat of arms over the
chimney, are these verses writ (as my lord told
me) by Lady Arabella, who was cousin to King
James :—

> Sanguine, cornu, corde, oculo, pede cervicis et aure
> Nobilis ; at claro pondere nobilior.

Aucupium.      A great help to the cymbal nets for bringing in
of larks about your net, is a gigg of feathers standing a distance off, which twirleth swiftly round on
the least breath of wind.    When the sun doth not
shine, a fox tail pulled up within the compass of
your net will make the larks strike at it as if it
were a weasel.

Dress lime-twigs by the fire ; anoint your
hands and your twigs a little with goose-grease,
or any such like thing ; cleanse your hands with
bran, &c.

You may take a hawk by turning out a bird
with a most slender limed twig ; lime the bird's
back, and that alone will entangle the hawk.

When you hear a pheasant crow, turn out near

to him a house-cock, which will answer the crowing of the pheasant, and thereupon they will meet and fight, so that you may take the pheasant with your hand.

My Lord Langdale (the first) bred up his children in much awe and fear. His eldest son, being then a father of many children, did observe him (even till my lord's death) with a childish awe. And though this son was a man of a high spirit, yet finding it to be, as he thought, ungrateful to his father, he durst not give him nor procure anyone to give him notice in his last sickness of the apparent signs of his death, so that my lord (who did not expect death) died without the help of a priest. His son, who lived in the house and durst scarce visit him in his sickness, did not so much as adventure to pray by his bedside till my lord was in his last pangs and not able to observe what he did. One of the family told me this, that was present at his death.

Liberorum educatio.

Sir Richard Houghton's daughter did fly from her parents and married a poor minister. The bustle she made to be got away was apparent to the servants, but no one durst speak a word, for

N N

my lady her mother, who had made her daughter the idol of the family, would never endure to hear anything said against her.

Praise your children openly, reprehend them secretly.

Sir Marmaduke Langdale, the famous Royalist leader, was created Baron Langdale of Holme, County York, in 1658. The austerity of his manner is spoken of by others. Lloyd describes him as a lean mortified man, so that his enemies called him the ghost. They had some reason for this, considering that he haunted them so much. He is highly commended by Clarendon, and is said to have spent 160,000*l.* in the King's service. He died at his seat, Holme, in Yorkshire, on August 5, 1661. His son Marmaduke, second Lord Langdale, was Governor of Hull for James II., and Mr. Blundell says that he was offered the command of a troop of horse, which he declined. The Barony became extinct in 1777 by the death of Marmaduke, fifth Lord Langdale, whose sister Mary had married Charles Philip, sixteenth Lord Stourton. Their third son, the Honourable Charles Stourton, assumed in 1815 the surname of Langdale only, in compliance with the will of Philip Langdale of Houghton, county York, Esq., to whose estates he succeeded. His honourable and religious character is well remembered, and on his death-bed he was admitted at his earnest desire into the Society of Jesus, putting on the habit of a lay-brother. The Cavalier's grandson, Nicholas Blundell, of Crosby, Esq., married in

1703 Frances, second daughter of Marmaduke, third Lord Langdale.

Sir Richard Hoghton, third Baronet of Hoghton, county Lancaster, was M.P. for his native county, and died February 1677–8. He had married Sarah, daughter of Philip, first Earl of Chesterfield, who survived him till 1698. This will be the lady referred to.

The casuists say it is not lawful to sell any- *Emptio et venditio.* thing above such or such a degree of dearness. Quære then, whether it be lawful to buy above such or such a degree of cheapness. If one may buy as cheap as he can, and yet may not sell as dear as he can, how comes this judgment to pass in favour of money? For he that giveth the money is called the buyer; he that giveth any other thing (I mean by such contract) is called the seller; whereas my horse doth buy for me my neighbour's money, as well as my neighbour's money doth buy my horse for him.

Cato counselled those that were to take a farm, to have a great regard what neighbours it had, and Themistocles, being to sell a certain manor, caused the cryers to proclaim that it had good neighbours.

A friend of mine, a person of great virtue, who *Duellum.*

N N 2

used to spend eight or nine hours each day in prayer and meditation, made a long relation to me, how valiantly his son had lately behaved himself in the acceptance of a duel.  He made little complaint against him, only (when I said so) confessed it was unlawful, yet it seemed very apparent that he took a kind of glory in his son's supposed gallantry.  So much doth false honour deceive even virtuous men.  For this same person was at that very time continuing in a long and great displeasure against a younger son of his own for having married below his quality, although the portion was really more than his own fortunes deserved.  So that it seems, if sins be fashionable sins, we cannot blame them.  We would not go to hell unless honour calls us.  Nay, we should be content to go to Heaven, if it were not against our credit to receive an affront.

Decimæ.

The tyrannical decimation of Cromwell is yet in fresh memory.  It was once conceived to be so firmly established, that a friend of mine took my 6*d.* to give me 10*s.* when the decimation should cease.  This he did soon after perform.  The decimation was laid upon us in the year 1655, and

taken off about two years later. Sir Wm. Petty,
in his book of taxes, proposes a way for the
saving of 500,000*l.* per annum of the Church
revenues of England, which being allotted for the
publick charge, the care of souls may, notwithstanding, be taken sufficiently by encouragement
for the remaining revenue.

1646.—My Lord of Derby took the custom of Epigramma.
some mills from Deemster Christian, and the Calf
of Man from Dick Stevenson, and after that
Stevenson and Will Christian feasted his Lordship:
on which was made this epigram—

> Will did invite his guests ; they eat their fill :
> He gave them bread that robbed his father's mill ;
> But was not Dick the madder man by half,
> To give him veal that stole away his calf?

1664, May 23.—Laurence Ireland, Esq., being Mirabilia
quædam ad
that very day aged thirty years, and left by the fidem spectantia.
late death of his wife a jolly, healthful widower
with two daughters and no son, told me as we were
coming from Holywell, that he would not marry
again, although by that marriage he should know
that all the people of England would become
Catholics. That day I took leave of him, who

was then on his journey towards the other side of
the sea with intention to undertake a religious life.

> Laurence Ireland of Lydiate, the last squire of
> his race, after the death of his wife, became a Jesuit,
> and died of consumption at York, June 30, 1673.
> He was an intimate friend and neighbour of Mr.
> Blundell, and entrusted his two young children to
> the care of his lady, to whom he writes afterwards
> in terms of grateful acknowledgment for the care
> bestowed upon them. He settled his estate of
> Lydiate Manor, &c., on his elder daughter Mar-
> garet, who married Sir Charles Anderton, second
> Baronet of Lostock, and had a numerous issue.
> The second daughter, Katharine, became a Nun
> O.S.B. at Dunkirk, where she died February 4,
> 1740. (See ' Lydiate Hall and its Associations.')

Morstin, &c.     A.D. 1660.—About the end of June, I met
with a young Polander at Dieppe, with whom I
had much free and pleasant company for sundry
days at the same inn.   He was newly landed from
his own country.   He spoke Latin most readily,
and learnt it (as he said) at seven years of age by
conversing with his father and a tutor.   He appeared to be little or no less than twenty-four years
of age, yet he told me he was born November 10,
1641, so that he had not then attained to the twen-
tieth year of his age.   If that was true, he was

almost prodigiously learned for one of that age. Sure I am he gaye me great occasion of humility. I could scarcely mention anything, even out of those Latin books which I had studied and pored on with endless repetitions, but he had it almost by heart ; or else knew the substance thereof much better than myself. Especially Barclay's ' Argenis,' the historical part of which I had read over no fewer than eight times. The like of ' Quintus Curtius,' &c. I never met with an Englishman that seemed to know the tenth part of what he knew and repeated to me of Owen, our English epigrammatist. Seneca the philosopher was his *vade mecum*, and he seemed to have sucked all the marrow out of that book. He wrote his name thus in my table-book, ' Stanislaus de Ratiborko Morstin." He said he was nephew to that Morstin whose name we often read in the newsbook as Secretary to the King of Poland. He wrote in my book sundry epigrams, one of which is as follows :—

In Reginam Poloniæ nomine, non re, Bonam.

Qui tibi cunque Bonæ sacris dum tingeris undis
Imposuit nomen, omnibus imposuit.

Treasure-
trove at
Scarisbrick.

Extract from a letter of William Blundell to Mr. Scarisbrick at St. Omers College, April 29, 1655:—Hugh Worthington, your tenant, hath found a few days since, in the ground about his house, divers scores of most ancient Roman pieces, many of them pure silver, others (supposed once to be gold) prove now but brass: these about half-a-crown in weight, those but sixpence. The faces and inscriptions upon the silver coin are clearly apparent, and very neatly cut ; the character is the same now used, or with little difference. One of these bears the face of Vespasian, with his name and title (Cæsar) stamped at large upon the verge. On the other side is a woman, despoiled of all her dresses, in a sedentary and pensive posture, and the inscription upon the ring, Judæa. You have in others S P Q R in a wreath of laurel, the Roman eagle displayed, the altars and instruments of sacrifice, with the faces of sundry of the first twelve Cæsars, no less discernible than the stamps of our modern coin. Thus, sir, you may see that your learned Worship's poor tenants, without the trouble of Livy, Tacitus, Suetonius, or any other of those crabbed companions, are as conversant with the noble old heroes as yourself. We have here an odd opinion, that the finding of iron is lucky, but of silver extremely unfortunate.

> James Scarisbrick of Scarisbrick, county Lancashire, was first cousin to the writer, their mothers being two sisters, daughters of Roger Bradshaigh of the Haigh, Esq. Mr. Scarisbrick succeeded his father Edward in the estate in 1653, at the age of eighteen, and had returned to St. Omers to finish his studies. He died of fever April 1673, and was the subject of the remarkable dream of Lady Clifton, related in another place, and told Mr. Blundell by Sir Thomas Clifton on the day of the funeral, May 1, 1673.

December 18, 1663.—Jack Hesketh, starting at the usual place of Crosby course, and running by Lightheeles stubb (left on the left hand) to Crosby pole, and turning back the very same way, came to the start again in twelve minutes and two-thirds of a minute, as near as I could hit it by the help of a half-quarter and a half-minute glass. The horse was the Earl of Derby's, matched to run for 100*l.* January 11 following, with a gray gelding to carry 15 stone 9 lbs., and the horse 12 stone 9 lbs. The rider abovesaid weighed, when he gave the heat, 12 stone 10½ lbs. ; he was shamefully beaten.

My blind stallion did run, by the same glasses, upon the sea sands (which were then heavy),

*Equorum cursus.*

running off and on, and turning in a compass of about 25 yards in diameter, just 5 miles and 82 roods.  Each rood is 24 feet, and each mile 220 roods, which is after the measure of 320 statute perch to a mile, each perch or rod consisting of 16½ feet.  He ran this space of ground in fifteen minutes time, wanting about the sixth part of one minute, and no more.

*Charitas.*    The news-book, August 24, 1665, tells how 'it hath pleased God to move the hearts of some citizens of London, &c. to consider of the great necessities of the poor of the out-parishes of this city, by reason of the dreadful visitation of the pestilence, and they have remitted the disposal of their charity to the Right Honourable Sir John Laurence, Lord Mayor of London.'  Then he tells us the just sum is 61*l*., and names twenty-five benefactors, beginning John Wiat, &c.  This I note as a ridiculous charity to be so published.

*Eleemosyna.*    John Widowes, the churchwarden of Winwick, when he opened the poor man's box which stands in the church, called upon the parson, Mr. Sherlock (a very charitable man) to be present at the opening of it, and withal said to him, ' Sir, if here be any brass money you ought to make it good.' ' Who, I ?' said Mr. Sherlock, ' I pray, sir, your reason.' ' Marry, sir,' replied Widowes, 'there is never a man but yourself that ever puts money into it, and therefore you ought to make it good if any be amiss.'

My aunt Massey used sometimes to give a peck or bushel of corn to several particular persons of the poorest sort. Once, when she had given a measure to a poor woman, the woman held her sack open after the corn was put in, and said, ' I hope, good Mrs., you will give me now some charity or overmeasure, according as others do after a measure of corn sold.'

I knew an old wandering beggar, by name Hesketh, of whom I have credibly heard this tale. He understood one time that a company of young gallants (most or all of them Catholics) were passing through Downholland, towards Scarisbrick. It was in the times of usurpation, and in the summer season. The man, being very old, had his grandson to attend him, whom he commanded to go aside ; then he threw himself into a puddle, and wallowed therein. The gallants, coming to the place, asked him what he was. He replied, 'I will never deny myself to be a Catholic, and because I am so, your comrades the troopers that went before you have beaten and used me thus ; and now I do expect you will kill me outright.' Hereupon the soft-hearted gallants made a contribution of twelve or fourteen shillings. Which when he had got, and the gentlemen passed away, he called to his boy and said, ' Here is a trick to help you when you grow to be old.'

Rev. Richard Sherlock, D.D., born 1612, was presented to the rectory of Winwick by Charles, Earl of Derby, and died June 16, 1689. He had the reputation of a pious, humble, and charitable man. The epitaph dictated by himself may still be seen in the chancel of that ancient church. It concludes with these words, 'Sal infatuatum conculcate ;' ('Tread under foot the worthless salt.') Dr. Sherlock's niece married Bishop Wilson.

The Masseys of Rixton Hall, near Warrington, were an ancient family, which became extinct in the male line about the middle of last century. The preceding anecdote regarding Dr. Sherlock would probably come to Mr. Blundell's knowledge through his relatives at Rixton.

Nimium nocet.

The golden mean is the best measure for all things ; and the hitting of this aright is the greatest wisdom. I fear my countrymen are not guilty of too much wit upon this account. We love all in excess. Our modes are now excessive little, then excessive large ; excessive broad and excessive narrow ; excessive long and excessive short ; extremely rich and extremely plain. The breeding of our children is and hath been faulty in the contrary extremes. The manners of wives for the most part are strangely changed. Once a velvet gown would have passed from mother to daughter for two or three generations, and they knew no more of London but only the name. Now they know the streets as well as the porters of the town ; and they pay not for their gowns and silk stockings till there be half-a-dozen on the score.

A while ago the best parts of the nation were given by pious souls into churchmen's hands, and a law was made to restrain these excessive gifts. Then presently comes a zeal which holds it a Christian work to destroy the Church and the churchmen. And because there was or seemed to be an excess before in some religious duties, the fonts were pulled down and the churches turned to stables.

Hiberni.

Mr. Richard Bellings in his letter to me, January 10, 1674, saith, 'I must say this for my nation, that next the Spaniard it is the laziest generation.'

Duodecim viri.

In August 1676, many great causes were brought into the Court to be tried, I being then at Lancaster, where I saw wretched mean persons most commonly (yea, almost wholly) upon the juries. Of these sundry were bum-bailiffs, as Tom Tilsley, Edward Atkinson, &c., whereof the latter was by far the best like man in the whole twelve. Sundry of these men served on twenty or thirty juries, and each had 4*d.* a piece in each cause. One John Brewer (who wants an eye) being then often sworn on the jury, a gentlewoman who stood next me (daughter to Mr. Rigby, Clerk of the Crown) told me that the said Brewer had two brothers who were drudges at her father's house and natural fools, and that the said John was little better; all which Mr. Rigby confirmed to me about two days after. Yet I saw this Brewer, and others that appeared as simple and as poor as he, sworn on the jury for the trial of Mrs. Anderton's estate in Lydiate, Melling, &c.,

which I take to be worth 10,000*l.* and more. Of
which jury young Mr. Preston of Holker was the
first, but no other like a gentleman except one,
Crowder. In this cause the plaintiff was non-
suited.

> The Mrs. Anderton, who had to defend her
> title to her estate under the disadvantages spoken
> of, was Margaret Ireland, who had married Mr.,
> afterwards Sir Charles Anderton, second Baronet of
> Lostock. Her father, Laurence Ireland, on leaving
> the world in 1664, had settled his estates upon her.
> After his death in 1673, they were claimed by his
> cousin Francis Ireland, who pleaded a settlement
> made by the grandfather in favour of the male line.
> Although this deed was recited at the Inquisition
> P. M., it was proved never to have been executed,
> so that the opposition fell to the ground. Lady
> Anderton enjoyed her estates till her death in 1720,
> when her bequest of them became the occasion of
> some curious proceedings. (See 'Lydiate Hall and
> its Associations.')

I am now (1676) eight or nine years older than *Patientia.*
Cato Uticencis was at the time of his death, yet I
never drew blood by giving a blow to a servant.
But Cato, the very next night before his designed
and much-famed death, blooded his own hand by
striking his servant even for a faithful and loving
act. Yet Cato was very patient, and I am a pas-

sionate wretch.  We are not to judge of men by
one act or circumstance.

Edvardi Scarisbrick, Armigeri, Lancastriensis,
Quod reliquum, hic situm est.
(&c.) Obiit November 7, 1652.

The above is engraven upon a square marble,
which I procured to be set in the church of St.
Andrew in Holborn, together with his coat of
arms.  You may find it over his grave, upon the
left hand as you enter at the little south gate.

There are nine eulogistic lines, in one of which
the deceased is described as dear 'to God, to the
Angels, and to Stanley' (Deo, Angelis et Stanlæo),
a curious climax, the conception of Rev. Samuel
Rutter, Chaplain to the Earl of Derby and afterwards Bishop of Sodor and Man, who composed
this inscription.  A friend who kindly undertook to
look for it in the present church informs the writer
that the ancient monuments are put together in an
ante-chapel under the tower.  He says that the
room is so dark and the monuments placed at such
a height, that it is difficult to see, and impossible to
decipher any inscription.  The church standing in
1652 escaped the fire, but did not escape the de-
stroying hand of Christopher Wren, by whom it was
rebuilt in 1686.  Hare ('Walks in London,' vol. ii.
p. 193) calls it a bad likeness of St. James', Picca-
dilly.  Its associations are not without interest.

Richard Savage, the Poet, was baptised there, and it was the burial place of the unfortunate Chatterton. Stillingfleet was its Rector in 1665, and later on, Dr. Sacheverel, whose name became the 'shibboleth' of a party. He died Rector in 1724, and lies buried in the chancel.

A former Edward Scarisbrick had been receiver-general for Henry, Earl of Derby, and was one of the gentlemen-ushers who attended the burial of his father Edward, Earl of Derby, in that remarkable display of funeral pageantry which the town of Ormskirk witnessed on December 4, 1574. The full details may be found in Collins' Peerage, which says that the place assigned by the Heralds to Edward Scarisbrick was to accompany the chariot which conveyed the body itself :

'Then the chariot, wherein the body lay, was covered with black velvet garnished with escutcheons, drawn by four horses, trapped with black, and on each horse was placed four escutcheons and a shaffron of his arms, and also on each horse sat a page in a black coat, and a hood on his head ; on the fore-seat of the said chariot sat a gentleman-usher in his gown, and his hood on his head, and a white rod in his hand ' (vol. ii. p. 76).

This Edward Scarisbrick, having lost his only son Alexander, left the property to his nearest heir-male, Thomas Scarisbrick of Borwick, in Furness, whose son Henry died in 1608. The latter was succeeded by his son Edward, the person commemorated by Mr. Blundell, whose uncle he was by marriage with Frances, daughter of Roger Bradshaigh of Haigh, near Wigan, Esq. The last in the male line of this ancient race was the late

Charles Scarisbrick, Esq., who died unmarried in 1860, leaving large possessions, inherited and acquired. The manors of Scarisbrick, Halsall and Downholland, fell to his eldest sister, Ann, widow of Sir Thomas Windsor Hunloke, of Wingerworth, Derbyshire, Bart., who assumed the name of Scarisbrick. At her death in 1872, she was succeeded by her only surviving daughter, Eliza Margaret, married to Leon Biandos, Marquis de Castèja. This lady is since dead without issue, and the Marquis now enjoys the estate.

Gelu.

I do not remember any frost in England so long and so violent as that which happened in the year 1683–4, concerning which I shall here insert some words out of Mr. Michael Rock's letter, dated at London, January 29, 1683, and directed to Edmund Butler, Esq., at Crosby, viz. :—

'We have but little news about town ; that which gives most occasion of discourse is the extremity of the weather, and our great river Thames being frozen over. The like was never seen, it being almost every day covered over with people ; several booths—nay, several thousands of booths are built on it, and coaches and carts go as frequently on it almost as in the streets. The common passage from the city to Whitehall and Westminster is on the Thames, it being the shorter cut.

We had yesterday a bull baited on the Thames. In fine, it looks like a vast common, and not a river. Every day for this month past, it seemed as if there were a fair upon it, all things being sold there in booths, of which there are several great lanes between the bridge and Westminster, besides what are all along up the river and below the bridge. The like was never seen by any man now living. All trade and commerce is ruined by this weather, for no posts can come or go. There is now due from Ireland thirteen packets, and five or six from other parts.'

On August 26, 1674, I was told at Dublin by one Mr. Carney (who lived, as I take it, at his own house, the Holy Lamb, in High Street), that he had seen the crosier staff of St. Patrick, which he saith is kept by Donogh, alias Denis Carney, of Ballidough, in the county of Tipperary. Alford speaks of this staff, tome 1, p. 539.

*Patricius Hiberniæ apostolus.*

There died in the compass of about one year four of our chiefest Lancashire colonels of the Parliament party, viz., Ashton, Dodding, More, and Rigby. Of which the last was thought, as his nephew told me, to be certainly poisoned.

*Parliamentarians and sequestrators.*

There died within the compass of seven weeks,
1656, Lieutenant Colonel Aspinwall, Colonel Holcroft, and Colonel Egerton, of which the last did
poison himself by mistake.   There died also a few
months before, Jo. Atherton, Esq., High Sheriff of
the county, who had been a captain for the Parliament.   Since the Great Committee for Sequestration was changed, there have been five new
Commissioners, four whereof, to wit, Holt, Cunliffe,
Massey, Aspinwall, are all of them dead, and had
the same precedence in death as they had in their
severity.   Mr. Pigot, indeed, who had left the place,
and was esteemed the most moderate of them all,
is yet alive.

The judgment that hath been shown upon
sequestrators hath been very observable, and no
less upon those that have intruded to other men's
estates.   Witness Mr. Ambrose, Ellison, Richard-
son, the man that expired in so horrid a manner
on the edge of Yorkshire, that other that was killed
with a tile, and the man that left the employment
upon the breaking of his leg.   These were all
sequestrators, but inquire further.

For intruders, there was Mr. Chorley, his
daughter, and others of his family that died in a

horrid manner. Then Norris, Whittson, Latham.
I have heard it confidently reported that Peter
Ambrose (that worst sequestrator of all others)
died of phthisis, being a prisoner to the State,
because he could not make his accounts.

Colonel Ralph Ashton, Major-General, and M.P.
for Lancashire, was of the Middleton branch of that
family. He is said to have died 1652, aged forty-
five. Colonel George Dodding was son of Miles
Dodding, of Conishead Priory, Lancashire, Esq., and
had commanded one of the Lancashire regiments
during the civil war. Colonel John Holcroft was of
Holcroft, Lancashire, and defended Lancaster Castle
against the Royalists in 1643. He was buried at
Newchurch, in Winwick parish, on April 22, 1656.
His daughter Mary married Colonel Blood.

Colonel Peter Egerton, of Shaw, near Flixton,
commanded the Parliamentary forces at the siege
of Latham House. From the Flixton register he
appears to have died May 22, 1656. In Newcome's
Autobiography, November 1657, we find the following reference to his death :—' This induces to re-
membrance another sad story that was notoriously
known not many years since of Colonel Egerton
of the Shaw, here in Lancashire, who used to take
flower of brimstone for some distemper he had, and
he sent the maid into the closet, and she mingled it
with milk, and he drunk it, and it proved mercury ;
and by this woful mistake he was poisoned, and died
within a few hours.' John Atherton of Atherton,
Esq., died January 17, and was buried at Atherton

January 24, 1655-6. In his funeral sermon, delivered by J. Livesey, minister of the Gospel at Atherton, he is extolled as one 'who in his youth was counted worthy of command in a valiant, victorious army.'

Alexander Norris, of Bolton, was treasurer of the Parliamentary Committee for Lancashire, in 1645. On April 1, 1643, Nicholas and Robert Cunliffe are both in the list of Lancashire sequestrators ; the former is said to be of Hollinge.  Peter Holt's name appears in 1649, and that of William Ambrose at an earlier date.  George Piggott was a Commissioner in 1650 ; Edward Aspinall and Ro. Massey, in 1654.— J. E. B.

Colonel John More was son and heir of Edward More, of Bank Hall, near Liverpool, Esq., who fell down dead in the street (as Mr. Blundell records) about 1632.  To Colonel More was entrusted the defence of Liverpool when besieged by Prince Rupert.  He conducted a force into Ireland at the time of Cromwell's expedition, and died at Dublin on his return in 1650.  He was M.P. for Liverpool, and one of those members who signed the warrant for the King's death.

There were three Colonels Rigby of the name of Alexander, all active partisans in the civil war.  The one referred to was of Middleton, and originally bred to the law.  Entering the army, he became one of its foremost leaders, and is styled by Lady Derby 'that inveterate rebel.'  He was M.P. for Wigan in the Long Parliament, and made a Baron of the Exchequer in 1649.  He died the following year at Croydon, while on the circuit, of an infectious disorder, to which both his companion Judge

Yates, and the Sheriff of the County fell victims.
His son Alexander was also a Lieutenant Colonel
for the Parliament, and is mentioned by Mr. Blundell
as having related to Mr. William Blundell, when
they met at Haigh, an anecdote already given. The
third, Colonel Alexander Rigby, was of the Burgh
family, and on the side of the King. It was his son,
Alexander Rigby, of Layton, who, when Sheriff of
Lancashire in 1677, erected the monument to Sir
Thomas Tildesley, which may still be seen on the
battle field, near Wigan, where that gallant hero
fell.

Mr. Blundell has the following notice at the end
of an obituary for 1679 : 'Evan Heaton, of Billinge,
an old sequestrator, drowned in a pit as he came
from Wigan, in the way from which he had drunk at
two ale-houses.'

I heard the Countess of Derby say, A.D. 1644, Miracula.
that since miracles ceased in the Church, she
thought there had not been a more wonderful
thing than the preservation of Latham House. It
was then newly relieved from a long siege in
which her Ladyship had made a most noble resistance.

It has been asserted by some writers that Mr.
Blundell himself took part in this memorable defence. This is clearly a mistake ; as the wound
which he received at the assault on Lancaster,
March 18, 1642–3, was of so severe a nature as to

render him totally incapable of any further active military service. Charlotte, Countess of Derby, died at Knowsley on March 22, 1663.

*Aucupium et variæ ejus artes.*

Observe a flock of stares (or shepsters) when they are ready to lodge themselves in a dovecote or some thicket, and you shall see how they will fly up and down together a long time in a great and thick knot. If you do then turn out a quick stare with a limed thread of near three yards long, she will straight fly to the rest, and flocking among them she will infallibly bring down entangled with her thread one or two (at the least) and perhaps five or six of those birds ; and this you may do often with the like success. But take heed that the thread be not limed too near the bird. This experiment has been tried successfully by Mr. Thomas Stanton, from whom I had it.

He told me of a merry conceited experiment (which I rather take to be a mere speculation) of catching wild ducks. If you go into the water up to the neck, with a pumpion put over your head, and whilst the ducks come to eat the seeds which must be stuck upon the outsides of the pumpion, you may take them by the legs, and pluck them quietly one after another under the water.

He told me likewise of an odd ridiculous way of catching herons, which I forbear to relate. October 29, 1660.

About the year 1648 or '49, I sowed cherry stones upon a garden bed finely wrought for that purpose. There came up no cherry tree at all, but in place thereof a pretty crop of ash plants, sundry of which were planted afterwards in the parsnip yard or dovecote croft, as we now call it. I do not doubt at all but that they were really produced of the stone of cherries, for no seeds of ashes were sown on that bed that I do know or suspect. And I do presume that the stones grew of such a tree as had been grafted in the stock of a cherry. For the seed of fruit will produce a tree agreeable to the stock or root from whence it came.

*Fraxinus ex cera-i semine nata.*

The following are the latest notes written by Mr. Blundell, and were compiled in answer to an application from some London booksellers for any remarkable facts suitable for a new edition of Camden's 'Britannia.' They were addressed in 1693, a portion of them to Mr. Abel Swall, Bookseller, at the Unicorn, at the West-end of St. Paul's, London, and the remainder to Mr. Timothy Childe, Bookseller.

Q Q

Altcar.

I find the township of Altcar &c. in Lancashire to have the privilege to be free from taxes, at the least from such as are laid for the behoof of the county.

Formby.

Mr. Camden speaks of fishes caught by the diggers within the earth. He calls the place Ferneby, but the name is certainly Formby. I have lived above sixty years in the neighbourhood, yet I can by no inquiry hear of any such thing. True it is that the unctuous matter he speaks of there is greatly remarkable. A chemist in our neighbourhood reports that he has extracted from it, being first congealed into a turf, an oil extraordinary sovereign for paralytic distempers, &c.

Lathom
spaw.

Mineral waters or spaws are now abounding everywhere in the kingdom. We have one of these in the Earl of Derby's ground near Lathom Park, Lancashire. The want of convenient lodging makes it less frequented, and I had not mentioned it but that it hath done some notable cures, and one to my certain knowledge the greatest and the quickest that ever I knew to be done by any such water.

I think you ought to inform yourself of that most wonderful mine of solid salt lately discovered in Cheshire. A lump of the same was given me by Sir J. P. and I can scarcely distinguish it from alum except only by the taste. It is said to be about forty foot thick, and certainly all the rich salt springs in the Wiches mentioned by Mr. Camden derive their perpetual flow from this or from such like.

The buildings and people of Leverpoole, our next post town, are certainly more than doubly augmented and the customs eight or ten-fold increased within twenty-eight years last past.

That heroic and loyal act of Sherlotta Countess of Derby in her personal and successful defence of Latham House against a potent and long siege in 1644 may deserve an entire history. It is true that that ancient house after a second siege was laid almost flat in the dust, and so was the head of James, that loyal Earl of Derby, cut off at Bolton in Lancashire October 15, 1651, by the rebels' prevailing power.

Lead mine.

A mine of lead in Whittle, near Chorley, Lancashire, lately found and wrought with good success in the land of Sir Ric. Standish, I take to be the first lead mine that has been wrought in this country.

Mill-stones.

Near to the same place is a plentiful quarry of mill-stones not less fit to be noted than that which is mentioned by Camden in the ' Peak.'

Iron.

Mines in Furness and elsewhere which produce iron-ore. I have seen one of them long since, but I know not how they succeed. I think they were not known in Camden's time.

Coal.

There are plentiful and profitable mines of an extraordinary canel-coal wrought now and long in the grounds of Sir R[oger] B[radshaigh] of Haigh, near Wigan. Besides the splendid flame it yields in burning, we have often seen this coal framed and curiously polished into the appearance of black marble and into the forms of large candlesticks, sugar-boxes, spoons and many other knacks to garnish as it were a cupboard with a kind of sable plate. These things have been a very acceptable present to our friends at London and to others beyond the seas.

Mr. Camden speaks of the prodigious floating of certain fatal blocks as predicting the death of the heirs of the family of the Breertons. I never heard the thing contradicted, saving that in a long discourse which an ancient lady of that house made of that subject to Sherlotta Countess of Derby, I heard her say that she did not give much credit to it. Yet she seemed to ground her disbelief too much upon one late imposture proved upon the boatmen of the place who had drawn much people together and gotten some money from them by playing a knavish trick. The truth of the main matter may be worth the search.

*Breerton prognostic.*

In 1646 I observed in the Isle of Man that a person who desired to commence a suit brought a small piece of slate or thin stone to the Governor, whereon he wrote his name or mark with a stile or such like matter and gave it back to the plaintiff. He was then pleased to tell me that this being delivered to the defendant imported as much as a summons under a penalty to appear in the Court.

*Isle of Man.*

This story may be pleasant enough to an Englishman that spends so much money in his proceedings
at law.

Northamp-
ton.

It may be noted upon the city of Northampton
that from the ancient rotten buildings of wood and
clay it has now become the handsomest little town
in the kingdom, and not unlike to the fine buildings in Holland.

Dublin.

Dublin is strangely beautified with building on
new ground and also with several bridges. The
bowling-green is highly pleasant, convenient, and
large. There I have seen eight companies or sets
of bowlers playing all at a time ; and the Lord
Lieutenant himself being one, it is not to be
thought he would suffer the ground to be cloyed.

Kilkenny.

The reason why the city of Kilkenny in Ireland is commonly said to have *water without mud,
air without fog, and fire without smoke*, is taken
from the limpidness of the river, the dryness of
the seat, and from that admirable hot-pit coal
which is hardly ever seen to blaze or smoke. The
castle peereth aloft delicately just over the river.

The following obituaries which Mr. Blundell has added to collections of his letters, may be useful in fixing dates and particulars of the deaths of remarkable persons :—

### 1672–3.

Mr. Moore dyed June 17. Mr. Thomas Moore dyed June 21. Mrs. Peters, of Greenfield. Mr. William Anderton. Elin Shepard. Ginet Hil. Mr. Fenwick Moore dyed June 28. Edmond Hulm. Captain Asmal, of Amerston. Lady Howard, of Corby. Mr. John Gerard and his only chyld. Catherine Bridge. My niece Clenel. Mr. Plumpton Atturney. Mr. Thomas Blundel, of Ince. Mr. Haskene, of Haskene, and (a few weeks after) his brother. Mr. Samuel Aspinwill. Mr. Raphael Hollinshead. Mr. John Vincent, alias Kanes. Mrs. Elinor Eccleston. Mrs. Catherine Shakerley. About eighty men drowned on Formby shore in a ship, September 22 or 23. Mrs. Elizabeth Ogles. Sir Cicil Traford. Mr. Sayers drowned a hunting at y$^e$ Breck, November 25. The Earle of Derby dyed at Knowsley of a dropsie, on December 21, 1672. Alderman Brownlow, of Leverpool, a young man who had been maior y$^e$ year before. Mrs. Townley, of Townley, a mother of many young children. At Leverpoole dead in

a few dayes three young men of note, Alderman
Brownlow, Mr. Robert Breers, merchant, and Mr.
Formby, newly marryed.   The Duke of Richmond
sodainly.   Sir George Midleton.   Mr. Farrington,
of Werden.   Mr. Marshal, of Prescot.   Mr. Charles
Walmsley, of Selby.   Sarracol (Sorocold) of —,
reported to be worth 26,000*l.*   Richard Adam.
Mr. Thomas Scarisbrick.   The Lady Haggerston.
The Roman Empres.   James Scarisbrick, Esq.
Young Mrs. Preston, of Howker (Holker).   Young
Mrs. Nowel, of Read.   Lady Mountgaret dyed in
February or March.   The Lady Shakerley.   So-
merset Oldfield, of Oldfield, Esq. dyed sodainly ;
so did Mr. Francis Hollinshead.   The Lady Preston.
Mr. Plowden, of Plowden.   Mrs. More, of Bank
Hall.   Mr. James Anderton, of Lostock, was slain
in the year 1672, in parting som persons that
fought.   My sister Haggerston, June 22, 1673, and
her onely daughter at y⁰ same hour.   Mr. Laurence
Ireland, June 30, 1673.   Mrs. Stanley, of Eccleston,
dyed in chyldbed.   Sir William Stanley, September 24, 1673.   Mr. Gerard P.

In the margin these notes are inserted :—

Mrs. Brigit Savage maryed.   Lady Stanley

distracted.    Mr. R. Bradshaigh    maryed.    Lady
Clifton's dream.    Jack Clifton's ruin.

1673-4-5.

November 1673, Mr. William Martin dyed
sodainly in drink at Leverpool.  James Anderton,
Esq. dyed December 16.   My aunt, Elin Bradshaigh, at Roan, December 28.   Mr. Robert Mayl.
Mr. Peter Stanley.   Mr. Andrew Holland.   Lame
Gervise Clifton.   Dutches of Newcastle.   Mrs.
Gorsuch.   About October 1673, Timothy, an old
huntsman of Sir Richard Fleetwood's (who was
well known at + B) fell from his horse as he came
from the ale-house in yᵉ evening, and was found
dead (unhurt, yet warm) in yᵉ morning, with yᵉ
whip in his hand.   Mr. William Parker, of Woof-
house.   Sir Thomas Haggerston, March 5, 1673
(or rather, perhaps, yᵉ 6th).   Mrs. Osbalston, of
Osbalston.    Mr. Richard Moore, P.    Mr. John
Mollins, P.   Mr. Staninought, parson of Aughton,
February 28, 1674.   John Tildesley.   Sir William
Stanley, of Hooton.   Mr. Edward Massey, of Pud-
dington.   Dr. Murton, parson of Sephton, February 28, 1674.   Mr. John Clifton.   Mrs. Westby,
of Burn.   Sir Gilbert Ireland dyed April 1675.

R R

Captain Peter Slater slain May 5. My Lady Ireland.    Mrs. Charles Westby.    Mrs. Clifton, of Litham.    Mr. Massey, of Rixton.    Mrs. Ogles, of Whiston.    Mr. John Tatlock.    Mr. Cuthbert Clifton, sen.    Mr. George Clifton.    Robert Hesketh, of Meales, Esq., in December 1675.    Mr. Holt, of Castleton.

The following notes occur in the margin :—

Mr. Parker lost the woof-house by a verdict at Lancaster.    Sir Thomas Preston entered into y$^e$ Novitiat of y$^e$ Jesuites, 1674.

### 1677–9.

Mr. Richard Ashton, of Littlewood, who had formerly slain two men in Lancashyre, was barbarously slain at London.    Sir Francis Anderton dyed at Parris, and his son Henry, in France.    Sir Richard Hoghton.    Thomas Arnold and William Hunt.    Mrs. Frances Latham.    Mr. H. Latham. Sir Edward More, October 4, 1678.    Mr. John Townley.    The only son of Sir Charles Anderton. Mr. Walmsley, in April 1679.    Mr. Bretherton, of y$^e$ Hey.    Mrs. Massey, of Rixton, May 10, 1679. Mr. Alcock, about March.    Mr. Gellibrond, of

Chorley, about June. Mrs. Elinor Anderton. Mrs. Elizabeth Anderton. Mr. John Cooke drowned in a ditch or pudle in December. Mr. Lancaster, of Rennel (Rainhill) about y$^e$ same time hardly escaped drowning, haveing fallen into a brook, out of which he got with much adoe, and died a few days after. Mr. Nich. Fazakerley, January 6, 1679. Mr. Robert Williamsō. Mr. John Leigh. Mrs. Singleton, of Steinig (Stayning). In or about Rainford, a maid having filled a pail of water at a pit, whilst she sat it on her head, fell back into y$^e$ pit and was drowned. Another girl or maid-servant in Rainford, on Thursday, January 29, 1679, fell into a pit and was drowned as shee was stooping to take water.

# INDEX.

LONDON : PRINTED BY
SPOTTISWOODE AND CO., NEW-STREET SQUARE
AND PARLIAMENT STREET

9 781845 748975